A Very Nervous Person's Guide to Horror Movies

A Very Nervous Person's Guide to Horror Movies

Mathias Clasen

OXFORD
UNIVERSITY PRESS

OXFORD
UNIVERSITY PRESS

Oxford University Press is a department of the University of Oxford. It furthers
the University's objective of excellence in research, scholarship, and education
by publishing worldwide. Oxford is a registered trade mark of Oxford University
Press in the UK and certain other countries.

Published in the United States of America by Oxford University Press
198 Madison Avenue, New York, NY 10016, United States of America.

Library of Congress Cataloging-in-Publication Data
Names: Clasen, Mathias, author.
Title: A very nervous person's guide to horror movies / Mathias Clasen.
Description: New York, NY : Oxford University Press, [2021] |
Includes bibliographical references and index.
Identifiers: LCCN 2021010152 (print) | LCCN 2021010153 (ebook) |
ISBN 9780197535899 (hardback) | ISBN 9780197535905 (paperback) |
ISBN 9780197535929 (epub)
Subjects: LCSH: Horror films—History and criticism. |
Horror films—Psychological aspects. | Fear in motion pictures. |
Motion picture audiences—Psychology.
Classification: LCC PN1995.9.H6 C518 2021 (print) |
LCC PN1995.9.H6 (ebook) | DDC 791.43/6164—dc23
LC record available at https://lccn.loc.gov/2021010152
LC ebook record available at https://lccn.loc.gov/2021010153

DOI: 10.1093/oso/9780197535899.001.0001

1 3 5 7 9 8 6 4 2

Paperback printed by LSC Communications, United States of America
Hardback printed by Bridgeport National Bindery, Inc., United States of America

To Joe Carroll, my friend and mentor

Contents

Preface

Thank you for picking up this book. I assume that you are a very nervous person with an interest in horror movies. Me, I'm a horror researcher . . . and a fairly nervous person, at least when it comes to horror movies. I will tell you what a horror researcher does in a moment, but first, I will say a little about nervousness.

Nervousness gets a bad rap, but if our species were not constitutionally nervous—an anxious hairless ape—we would not be here today. *Homo sapiens* has fought its way through millennia of life-or-death struggle. Our ancestors traversed jungles teeming with hungry cats and sneaky serpents, they crossed deserts under the unforgiving glare of a prehistoric sun, and they sailed across restless oceans inhabited by huge, barely glimpsed beasts. Without some vigilance, some nervousness, our species would not have made it. Of course there is such a thing as too much nervousness. Some people are so nervously inclined that their anxiety gets in the way of their pursuit of happiness. But moderate anxiety is not necessarily a bad thing.

As I am writing this, in the summer of 2020, it seems that we are all chronically nervous. Anxiety is not just simmering, it is boiling. The novel coronavirus, SARS-CoV-2, is cutting a swath of destruction across the planet. If that were not enough, we are facing increasing political polarization and civic unrest, irreversible climate change, a biodiversity crisis, and other such items from Pandora's Big Box of Very Bad Stuff. The future seems to be harder to predict than ever before, and we humans detest the unknown. Fear of the unknown is, as one psychologist puts it, the "one fear to rule them all."[1]

With all this anxiety and nervousness going around, why would you want to read about—let alone watch—horror movies? Well, many people like to play with fear. Our species' fearfulness is not only key to our success in terms of survival, it is also the engine in a range of leisure activities, from extreme sports over scary entertainment to frightening pretend play. Endlessly innovative, we humans have found a way to wring pleasure from our constitutional anxiety. I will be arguing in this book that we can get more than mere pleasure and diversion from horror movies—indeed, horror fiction may be a primary means through which we confront fear and anxiety. Recent research actually suggests that people who regularly watch horror movies are coping better with the COVID-19 pandemic than those who stay away from horror movies. It looks like habitual horror watchers are doing a better job of keeping negative emotions on a leash, maybe because they have more practice regulating their own fear and anxiety to keep from being overwhelmed by scary movies. (I will return to that research later in the book.)

As a horror researcher, I am interested in what horror is and what it does. My primary training is in literary and film study, and I work in an English department at Aarhus University, a large research university in Denmark. Most of my career has been dedicated to theoretical and interpretive work, but in recent years I have been branching out into more empirical work—collecting data, working with human subjects, measuring behavior and physiology, that sort of thing; all in an attempt to get deeper into the psychological machine room of the horror genre. I am lucky to have some brilliant colleagues who have been collaborating with me, and I recently received a large research grant from the Independent Research Fund Denmark to establish the Recreational Fear Lab. You can visit our homepage at www.fear.au.dk if you are interested in following our research.

Horror fascinates me because it is so paradoxical. Why would anybody in their right mind seek out entertainment designed to make them feel bad? And what does it *do* to them, this immersion in fictional universes that brim with blood, gore, and hairy monsters? What does horror *mean*? The roots of my professional interest in horror are in my own personal history. My childhood feelings toward horror were deeply ambivalent, but they morphed into full-blown fascination in my adolescence. I still cannot watch a horror movie alone, but I have grown to love the stuff. I hope to convey some of that enthusiasm, but that is not my main mission with this book.

The main mission is to train the searchlight of science on a number of concerns my nervous reader might have about horror movies.

Before I began writing the book, I collected information on the kinds of concerns people have about horror movies via informal surveys on social media. For instance, I would ask on Twitter or Facebook about what made people nervous about scary movies. I looked for patterns in the information I received, and found that a *lot* of people are curious yet nervous about horror—and that certain concerns loom large.

The jump scare, for instance, is mentioned very often. Lots of people dread the jump scares that have become so common in horror movies. They do not like being blindsided by a massive shock to the system. As one respondent wrote, "I hate [jump scares] so much I get angry just thinking about the worst ones I've experienced." That is maybe a fairly trivial concern, compared to another high scorer: concerns about one's mental or physical health. As one respondent puts it, horror movies "provide imagery for my brain to throw back at me when I'm feeling scared, e.g. when I'm walking home alone or looking out of a window when it's dark outside. This can be years later!" But can horror movies really traumatize you? Can you pass out or even die from horror movie fright?

Some people also expressed concerns over children watching horror movies. Can that be good for them? Will it make them unempathetic or violent? Others, in turn, wondered whether horror movies might not be immoral, dwelling as they often do on evil and nastiness. And some speculated that the current explosion of horror movies might be a symptom of a sick society. Finally, some folks were worried about looking stupid if they admitted they liked to watch horror, suggesting that the genre may have an image problem.

I spent the next year and a half or so reading up on the research that bears on these issues and writing this book. You may be surprised to learn that there is not *that* much empirical research on horror. For a genre that is so pervasive and popular, you would think that researchers had charted and explained every nook and cranny of the phenomenon. That is not the case. There is still a lot that we do not know about the psychology and biology of horror. We do know a fair amount about its potential negative effects—back in the 1980s, several teams of media psychologists conducted study after study on horror's traumatic potential, especially for young people—and there is plenty of psychological research that indirectly throws light on horror. So we are not completely in the dark, either. In this book, you will get a state-of-the-art sketch of the science of horror and advice on how to get through a horror movie with body and soul intact.

The book is guided by a particular perspective—my perspective, which is a distinctly Western perspective. Almost all of the movies I discuss or refer to in the book are canonical American horror movies, such as *The Exorcist* and *Halloween*. They are movies that I know very well since most of my research has been on American cinematic and literary horror, and which I assume my reader will be familiar with, or at least will have heard of. Despite this bias in perspective, I believe that my claims about the psychology of horror generalize to non-Western contexts. Horror movies across cultures use similar techniques to achieve similar aims, and people everywhere respond in similar ways to cinematic frights. Horror movies everywhere aim to scare audiences, and they do so by portraying some kind of danger—a dangerous person, animal, monster, or nonmaterial entity such as a ghost or demon. A Japanese cinema patron does not mistake *The Exorcist* for a comedy or a romance, and an American does not mistake *Ringu* for one either. Of course there are subtle differences in how people respond to scary movies, both cultural and individual, and I will discuss some such differences in this book. My main concern, however, is the commonalities—how people *tend* to respond to a jump scare, say, or how *most* people will react to a grisly depiction of disembowelment.

The book is organized so that each chapter addresses one main concern to emerge from my survey and subsequent research. Although many of the studies I discuss in the book are very technical, I have tried to write about them in an accessible language so that nonscientists should have no trouble coming along for the ride. (You will find references to scientific and scholarly studies throughout the book—if you want to track down the studies I refer to, just follow the notes.) Still, I think you will find something of interest even if you are a scientist or, indeed, a horror specialist. In writing this book, I was hoping not only to provide interesting information to the nervous person with little horror experience—I was hoping also to engage horror buffs and even people who would never watch a horror movie, but who have a relative or friend who is into that stuff and therefore want to understand what the big deal is and whether they should be concerned about that relative's or friend's mental or spiritual health.

Now, I am not going to tell you that you should not be nervous at all. Nervousness in moderation is a good thing, as I said—it keeps us alert and alive. And horror movies may also be a good thing, but in moderation. If you watch nothing but horror movies from sunup to sundown, day in and day out, you are probably going to become a little wobbly. But the occasional horror movie provides a healthy jolt to the system, not unlike taking a shot of ginger. As my own and others' research suggests, horror movies can help you confront anxieties, they have a surprising potential for bringing people together, they can be a stimulus for personal growth, and they can give you real insight. As the esteemed horror and fantasy film director Guillermo del Toro says, "To learn what we fear is to learn who we are."[2] Horror can tell us interesting things about human nature and culture. And, of course, horror movies can be a hell of a lot of fun.

1

What's the Big Deal about Horror Movies, and Who Watches Them, Anyway?

Imagine an alien anthropologist coming to visit Earth. Yeah, I know. "The seventies called, they want their hoary pop-science conceit back." Indulge me for a moment.

So our alien anthropologist has come to Earth, and she is documenting the behavior of this curious bipedal ape, *Homo sapiens*. Curious, yes, but not inexplicable. Human behavior makes sense to our alien anthropologist because human behavior follows the universal Darwinian laws of evolution, and her civilization discovered those laws a long time ago. Humans are biological organisms, just like flatworms and butterflies and extraterrestrials. Humans are even distantly related to the cotton plants from which they fabricate those garments that they use to cover their reproductive organs and protect themselves from the elements. Humans—like flatworms, butterflies, aliens, and cotton plants—evolved in an adaptive relationship with their environments. Evolution thus shaped them to act in ways that promote their genetic fitness, ways that increase their odds of surviving and reproducing.[1] In this, humans are like all other organisms.

The earth is a fairly hospitable place for humans, so far as terrestrial planets go, with plenty of resources—but it is hardly without danger. There are big, ape-eating predators roaming the continents, and there is a surprisingly diverse array of microorganisms that are dangerous to humans. Humans worry about those things. They find the predators frightening and the microorganisms scary and disgusting. They also worry about other humans assaulting them. They are fearful apes, and our alien anthropologist knows fear. She understands that, from an evolutionary perspective, fear is useful. Fear motivates an organism to stay clear of dangerous things. It is an inherently unpleasant emotion that packs a serious motivational punch. She knows that in a dangerous world, a fearless organism is soon enough a dead organism.

One day, however, she discovers something weird. She comes across a group of humans gathered in a big, dark room. They all sit facing the same direction, staring at a vertical surface on which are displayed patterns of flickering light. Artificial sounds are projected into the room from electroacoustic devices. The humans behave fearfully, as if they were in imminent danger. They exhibit behavioral signs of acute distress, emitting high-pitched warning calls and using their forelimbs to protect vital organs from assault. But there is no visible danger—no ape-eating predators in the room and apparently no significant concentration of pathogens. After about 90 earth minutes, the flickering lights die out and the artificial sounds disappear. The humans stop acting as if they were in danger. Oddly, they seem to be bonding intensely, exchanging verbal information in a pleasantly agitated way. What's going on?

A bit of research tells our anthropologist that these humans were watching something called a horror movie, which is a make-believe representation of a threat scenario. Humans, it turns out, find great pleasure in make-believe. The anthropologist cross-references her notes on human behavior with earthling scientific publications and learns that humans are highly imaginative apes. They have a brain mechanism that evolved to create imaginative scenarios—a kind of virtual reality device inside their heads.[2] Humans build whole worlds—sometimes wildly implausible worlds—within their own minds. They also use the mechanism to immerse themselves in make-believe worlds that *other* humans have constructed and conveyed through some communicative medium—language, for instance, or a combination of light and sound.

The anthropologist comes to understand why humans would find pleasure in immersing themselves in made-up worlds that are full of suspense, adventure, and romance. The sheer amount of time that humans spend in imaginary worlds seems a little frivolous to her alien mind, but she can see why that old Darwinian process would have hardwired humans to find pleasure in make-believe. It allows them to have all kinds of useful vicarious experiences, such as secondhand explorations of the vagaries of mate choice and of the subtleties of socializing. Still, why would they find *frightening* made-up worlds, such as those depicted in horror movies, appealing?

Horror movies, our anthropologist learns, can be defined as the kind of narrative fiction film that is designed to stimulate negative human emotions such as anxiety, dread, disgust, fear, horror, and terror. The genre overlaps with other kinds of films that humans are attracted to, such as thriller and fantasy films. But when humans talk about horror movies, they usually have in mind the kind of movie in which horror elements dominate, the kind of movie that tries to frighten the audience. It does so by inviting the viewer to become imaginatively immersed in a threat simulation—a virtual scenario that brims with fear- and disgust-evoking stimuli. Those stimuli tend to reflect the dangers that the human species has faced over evolutionary time, which is why there are so many predatory monsters, disgusting zombies, and reptilian agents of evil in the genre. The big monsters with their sharp muzzles and homicidal intentions, the nasty zombies that leave behind them trails of decomposing meat, and the serpentine agents of evil slithering through popular culture—all of those creatures exploit humans' evolved fear and disgust systems. So does the genre as a whole.

Maybe, our alien anthropologist muses, the paradoxical appeal of threat simulations is not really that paradoxical after all. Humans may use those threat simulations to learn about the dangers of their world. If humans find pleasure in threat simulations, they may be better equipped to survive and reproduce because they will have a mental database of secondhand information about danger, she thinks. (And don't worry, we are leaving her behind now. She has served her purpose and we wish her safe intergalactic travels.)

The aim of this book is to see what cutting-edge research can tell us about the peculiar phenomenon of horror movies and to scrutinize the many myths and misunderstandings that cling to the genre like flies to an undead body. First, though, we will take a look at the audience of horror movies.

Who Watches Horror Movies?

Imagine a horror movie buff—the kind of person who can quote dialogue from obscure slasher movies and who knows *exactly* what to watch on Netflix when you get together for a fright night of horror movie socializing. Who do you see before you? Man or woman, young or old? If you are like most people, you probably visualize a fairly young guy.

I often talk to people who believe that horror is a predominantly male genre. In fact, that seems to be the general perception—just like it is the general perception that the rom-com is a predominantly female genre. A German study set out to investigate such perceptions.[3] The researchers asked a bunch of undergraduates about their views on gender and movie genre preference. The undergrads were asked to rate movie genres on a scale from 0 to 10, where 0 indicated a genre that is "exclusively preferred by women" and 10 indicated a genre that is "exclusively preferred by men." The results were then averaged. For horror, the score was 6, meaning that at least this particular population of German undergrads—male as well as female respondents—see horror as a genre that is slightly more appealing to males than to females. For comparison, romance flicks scored about 1.5 and war movies about 8. The genres perceived to be most gender-neutral were crime and mystery.

So much for perceptions. What about reality? The science is pretty consistent. Study after study finds that males are slightly more likely than females to enjoy horror.[4] For example, a recent study—conducted by myself, the media researcher Jens Kjeldgaard-Christiansen, and the personality psychologist John A. Johnson—found such a slight difference.[5] I say slight, and I want to emphasize that the gender difference is tiny. Statistically significant, yes, but much smaller than many would assume. As you can see from the graph (Fig. 1.1), females tend to report slightly less liking of horror than males, and they say that they consume horror slightly less frequently than males. They also report that they prefer slightly less scary material than males, and they are a good deal more likely to say that they are easily scared by horror.

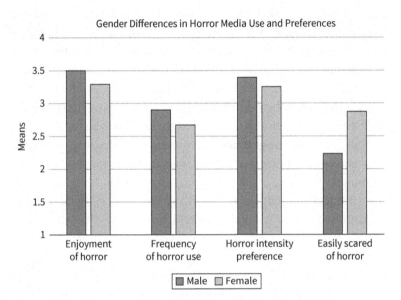

Figure 1.1 A big survey on horror movie preferences revealed some interesting gender differences: men are slightly more likely to say that they like horror, want their horror to be slightly more frightening, watch horror movies slightly more often, and are less likely to be easily scared by horror. The study collected data by having participants respond to different statements about horror media use and preferences. For example, participants would indicate the degree to which they agreed with statements like "I tend to enjoy horror media" (from 0, meaning "I strongly disagree," to 5, "I strongly agree"). They were also asked how often they had experienced horror entertainment in the past year (from 0, never, to 6, several times a week), and how intense they want their horror to be (from 1, "Not at all frightening," to 5, "Extremely frightening").

What explains this slight gender difference in horror preference and patterns of consumption? We think it has to do with underlying gender differences based in both biological and social factors. Psychological studies have found that females are biologically predisposed to react more strongly to negative stimuli.[6] They tend to be more prone to anxiety, and they consistently score higher on disgust sensitivity, meaning that they are more easily grossed out than men.[7] This makes sense in evolutionary terms. Males, on average, are stronger and more aggressive than females, and more likely to engage in violent conflict. That has been the case throughout human evolutionary history. They tend to pursue risky activities, not least as a strategy to attract mates, and so need lower baseline fear levels. Females, in contrast, evolved relatively high disgust levels as protection against infection (of themselves and any unborn child they might carry). That is the theory, at least. Whatever the cause, those gender differences in anxiety and disgust sensitivity seem to be universal.

Now, fear and disgust are both useful adaptations, as I have suggested—they protect us from dangers, such as the danger posed by hungry predators or infectious microorganisms—but there is always a trade-off. Imagine a human ancestor with extreme fear and disgust levels. That individual would never leave the homestead, never seek out new experiences, never meet new people, never pursue sexual encounters. That individual, in other words, would be poorly adapted—an evolutionary dead end.

So for millions of years of evolution, the forces of natural and sexual selection have hammered our species into shape, and we have these forces to thank for the statistical gender differences in fear and disgust sensitivity. Cultural forces interact with biological ones, and it seems plausible that women are typically socialized to be more willing to exhibit fear, for example. So when the women in our study were much more willing to admit that they were easily scared by horror, the reason is probably that women are biologically disposed to be more fearful *and* socialized to believe it is okay to admit when you are scared. Horror trades in frightening and often disgusting material, thus turning off a slightly larger proportion of women than men, apparently.

Aside from gender, are there other individual differences that may help explain why some people enjoy horror movies more so than other people? In the study that I mentioned before, we set out to investigate whether certain personality traits correlate with a tendency to enjoy horror.[8] We had our respondents—more than a thousand of them—fill out a long questionnaire that included questions designed to probe horror media use and preferences as well as personality characteristics. Our first interesting find was that the majority of our sample said that they liked horror. About 55% said that they agreed or strongly agreed with the statement "I tend to enjoy horror media." Only 14% strongly disagreed with that statement. (Another 14% just disagreed. The remaining 17% neither agreed nor disagreed, whatever that means. Maybe they were on the fence.) A fondness for horror, in other words, is not a minority phenomenon—quite the opposite.

We also did find that certain personality traits are correlated with a preference for horror. People who score highly on a personality trait called "imagination/intellect," in particular, are likely to report that they like horror. Such people enjoy intellectual stimulation and cognitive exploration. They like new adventures and experiences. Similarly, people who score highly on the trait "sensation-seeking" are likely to enjoy horror. Such people are easily bored and enjoy novel and intense experiences, such as extreme sports. They are also likely to enjoy risky experiences. However, these are not very strong correlations. It is perfectly possible to dislike intellectual stimulation and adventure and still be an avid horror fan. On average, though, typical horror fans probably enjoy new experiences that stimulate their minds no less than their nervous systems.

Is our typical horror fan of a particular age? One survey found that cinema audiences for horror movies in the UK are overwhelmingly made up of young people—52% were in the 15–24 age range, with another 24% in the 25–34 age range.[9] In our study, we did find a weak negative correlation between age and horror liking. In other words: the older somebody is, the less likely they are to enjoy horror. The age range is restricted in our study, however, because we only sampled individuals at least 18 years old. Other studies have found a so-called curvilinear relationship between age and horror liking. The communication scientists Joanne Cantor and Kenneth Levine published a meta-analysis of existing research and reported that the appetite for horror tends to increase in childhood, peak in adolescence, and slowly decline thereafter.[10]

This pattern, too, makes sense from an evolutionary perspective. Historically, adolescence is when people meet the world on their own and need to test their mettle. The appetite for exploration is particularly strong then, and adolescents are strongly motivated for finding and challenging boundaries (their own, as well as those of others, as anybody with a teenager in the house knows). It is when the appetite for thrills and risky behavior peaks.[11] It is not that children are uninterested in scary stories—far from it. But there is a reason why horror movies are not normally screened in nurseries and kindergartens, and we will get back to that in a later chapter.

So you may have to revise your idea of a typical horror movie enthusiast. He is not necessarily an unwashed, goateed twenty-something drooling over slasher movies in a basement man-cave adorned with Iron Maiden posters and Leatherface figurines. He may not even be a he. Might not be young, might not be a jittery thrill seeker or somebody with a stainless-steel nervous system. In fact, there are many different kinds of horror movie fans (including stereotypical ones). Young, old, female, male, anxious, fearless, imaginative, introverted, extraverted, you name it.

There are also different reasons for being a horror movie enthusiast. Some are social horror viewers. They are mainly in it for the intense socializing a horror movie can produce, during as well as after the experience. Going through something horrible yet fun together can have a powerfully bonding effect, as we'll see in a later chapter. Some watch horror primarily for the stimulation. The scarier, the better. Such horror enthusiasts have been dubbed "adrenaline junkies" by researchers. Others, the "white-knucklers," also enjoy horror, but for them, it is not a matter of maximal stimulation—it is a matter of keeping fear at a tolerable level.[12]

Along with two colleagues, Marc Andersen and Uffe Schjoedt, I did a study in a Danish haunted attraction, Dystopia Haunted

House.[13] We asked the visitors if they wanted to participate in our study (we paid for their ticket if they said yes). We then asked them to choose one of two challenges: to either try to maximize their own fear or try to minimize their own fear. As it happened, about half our sample—131 visitors—chose the minimize-fear challenge. We figure that those are the white-knucklers. The rest, 149 participants, went for the maximize-fear challenge—those, we think, are the adrenaline junkies. After participants had completed the haunted attraction, we asked about their fear and enjoyment levels, and also about the strategies they had used to meet the challenge (such as covering their eyes to keep fear down, or telling themselves that the scary monsters were real to increase fear).

Strikingly, our white-knucklers managed to keep fear at a significantly lower level than our adrenaline junkies, but both groups reported equally high levels of enjoyment. In other words, some people (the white-knucklers) find pleasure in the challenge of keeping their fear at a tolerable level while undergoing a horror experience, while other people (the adrenaline junkies) find pleasure in the challenge of being maximally frightened by such an experience. People can enjoy horror for different reasons.

How Popular Are Horror Movies?

Horror movies figure prominently in the pop-cultural landscape. Any respectable streaming service has a horror section (just like video rental stores had back in the day), and you can regularly find new horror movies at the multiplex. One curious exception is airline movie programming. There are very few horror movies in those in-flight entertainment systems. According to one estimate, horror movies make up only about 1% of in-flight programming.[14] Why? Well, a lot of people are anxious about flying and probably do not need an additional jolt to the fear system. Also, airlines do not want to offend passengers, and as we will see in a later chapter, horror has been known to offend folks. Finally, the passengers sitting next to you can see what is on your screen. Not necessarily an ideal situation if you are enjoying *Cannibal Hookers* with an excitable preteen to your left and to your right an octogenarian with one foot in the grave.

The horror genre goes back to the earliest days of cinema.[15] One of the first films ever made—a 14-minute silent picture produced in 1910 by Thomas Edison's production studio—was an adaptation of *Frankenstein*. American horror cinema began to take off in the 1930s, with the classic monster movies released by Universal Studios, such as Tod Browning's *Dracula* from 1931 and James Whale's *Frankenstein* from that same year. There was a steady increase in the production of horror movies across the twentieth century—to say nothing of the current millennium, which has witnessed an unprecedented glut of scary flicks. How many horror movies are there, and how has the number of horror movies produced changed over time?

To get an answer to those questions, I consulted the Internet Movie Database (IMDb). It turns out that more than 10,000 horror movies were made between 1900 and 2019. And those are only American, English-language, feature-length horror movies (or at least movies with a "horror" genre tag, so also genre hybrids such as horror comedies and action horror). However, that number includes some very obscure, even dubious titles—movies very few people have ever seen, not even (and maybe especially not) the director's mom.

So to get a better picture of the number of horror movies released in the period, I asked the search engine to filter out all movies that have been rated by fewer than 50 users. I figured this would eliminate, for example, amateur movies screened for family members and voted for by college buddies. Not that such movies cannot be interesting, but I was hoping to get a snapshot of reasonably professionally made American horror movies. With that added restriction, the number dropped to 6,315. Interestingly, most of the eliminated movies are pretty new. With the search restriction, I lost 12% of horror-tagged movies from 1900 to 1999 and an astounding 47% of movies from 2000 to 2019. A lot of the newer movies have very few votes. That is probably mainly because digital recording equipment has become incredibly cheap—anybody with a smartphone can shoot a film nowadays. There are more amateur horror movies now than ever before.

So, 6,315 movies made in the period 1900–2019. That is an average of one horror movie per week, across that whole period. To put the number of horror movies into perspective, IMDb lists a total of 38,827 American feature films in the English language with at least 50 votes across the same period. The proportion of movies with a "horror" tag across that whole period, then, is 16%. That is a respectable chunk.

Those thousands of horror movies are not spread out evenly across the whole period, though. As you can see in the graph (Fig. 1.2), horror movie production has increased dramatically, especially since mid-century. The *proportion* of horror relative to other genres has gone up too. In the year 2017, for instance, 339 out of a total of 1,283 movies had a "horror" tag. That amounts to 26%—a more than respectable chunk.

Now, these numbers are not the result of a scientific study; they are just an approximation. IMDb's genre tagging can be iffy. Sometimes a movie that is broadly considered to belong in the horror genre is

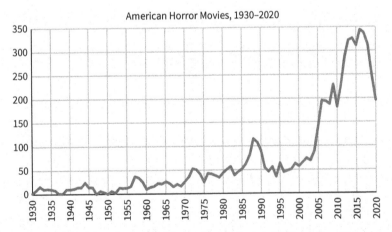

Figure 1.2 Horror movie production spiked in the late 1980s and really took off a few years into the new millennium. This graph shows the number of American horror movies produced in the period 1930–2020, according to the Internet Movie Database (IMDb). Movies made before 1930 are left out because there are very few of them. To filter out the most obscure titles, only movies with more than 50 user votes on IMDb are included.

assigned the "thriller" tag, but not the "horror" tag—*The Silence of the Lambs*, for example, and *The Sixth Sense*. Such movies would be left out of my search results. However, some movies that are not bona fide horror movies, but which may have horror elements, are included. So maybe in the end these two sets balance each other out. At any rate, these numbers give an indication of the sheer prominence of horror in cinema—and of the explosive development in horror movie production. There really are *lots* of scary movies out there.

The Big *Why?*

If you ask horror enthusiasts why they watch those movies, they will probably say it is because they think it is fun, or enjoyable, or some other synonym of *rewarding*. That goes for the adrenaline junkies, the white-knucklers, and the social horror watchers. Well, most of them, anyway. In our study on personality and horror, 81% of our respondents said that they had experienced horror media several times or more often over the last year. However, recall that about 55% agreed with the statement "I tend to enjoy horror media." So a good chunk of this sample—about a fourth—reported having watched horror even though they do not like it.

What gives? Maybe it is peer pressure. That has certainly been known to be a factor, especially among teenagers getting together to watch movies. Somebody suggests a horror movie, somebody else expresses disinclination, and everybody else goes "Cheep-cheep." Maybe it is also that for some people, the pleasure of socializing around a horror movie outweighs their displeasure at the movie itself. I think my wife would fall into that latter category. When the rest of the family is clamoring for a horror flick, she usually gives in and patiently watches right along with us whatever gore-filled shock-show we have picked out—sometimes between fingers or from behind a pillow, it is true, but that still counts.

The question remains: why would it be rewarding for *most* people to engage with a film that is designed to elicit negative emotion in the audience? Philosophers, scholars, and scientists have struggled with that question for a very long time. The ancient Greek philosopher Aristotle grappled with the paradox of tragedy—the pleasure people take from tragic stories. Aristotle's idea was that tragedy cleanses the mind of emotions such as pity and fear. He termed that phenomenon *catharsis*.[16]

If we take the idea literally and apply it to horror, the hypothesis would be that horror cleanses people of fear and anxiety. It does not look like people become less fearful after watching a horror movie, though. In our study on personality and horror, we asked respondents about changes in their anxiety levels after watching horror media because we wanted to probe the catharsis hypothesis. As it turned out, most respondents—52%—reported feeling *more* scared after watching horror, not less scared. They certainly were not purged of fear, since 42% reported no change. Only the remaining 6% said they felt less scared after watching horror.

So catharsis—at least in a literal interpretation—does not dissolve the paradox of horror. People do not seek out horror movies because they expect those movies to purge them of fear. In fact, people *want* the fear. It is not an unfortunate byproduct or a price you have to pay for whatever could conceivably be the primary attraction of horror. No, the fear itself is integral to the attraction of horror. In our study, we asked people how frightening they wanted their horror to be, on a scale ranging from "not at all frightening" to "extremely frightening." Only 4% said "not at all frightening"; 16% chose the "extremely frightening" option. But most people, about 80%, clustered in the moderately to highly frightening range.

People want the fear, and horror media are often marketed on their ability to generate fear, just as horror fans often point to the scariness of a horror film as an indication of quality. The theatrical trailer for the 2007 movie *Paranormal Activity*—one of the most commercially successful horror films of all time—showed a test audience responding to the film with extreme fear. "One of the scariest movies of all time," bragged the trailer. In 2016, the company behind the horror video game franchise *Outlast* launched an "adult diaper" campaign. Customers could buy a pair of Underscares™ in preparation for the involuntary bowel movement that might result from the second and allegedly extremely frightening game in the series. In 1958, the director of the horror film *Macabre*, William Castle, took out life insurance policies on his audience in case of death by fright. Nobody did die, but had they kicked the bucket during the film, their bereaved ones could have cashed a $1,000 check from Lloyd's of London (Fig. 1.3).[17]

If it is not catharsis, what then? A fairly common idea seems to be that horror movies are primarily about stimulation—that horror viewers basically want intense physiological arousal. They want their nervous systems dripping with adrenaline, they want their pulse through the roof, they want to feel alive. That is probably true for many horror fans, but it cannot be the whole story. There are much easier ways to self-stimulate than to sit through a two-hour movie (let alone a 30-hour survival horror video game or a 900-page novel by Stephen King). You could zap yourself with a mild electrical current or chug a bottle of hot sauce. You could ask somebody to awaken you from a nap with an air horn. All of that is stimulation.

Horror movies, at least good ones, offer more than physiological arousal. There is the suspense and the anxiety and all the other emotions, and there is the pleasure of absorption and of engagement with interesting characters. There may be thought-provoking subtext and prompts for moral reflection. Some of the best horror movies have intricate structures of meaning. You can't say that for being blasted awake by an air horn.

I believe that the threat simulation theory of horror, which I introduced earlier by way of our alien anthropologist, is a more complete and satisfying explanation for the peculiar appeal of horror.[18] When we watch a horror movie, we essentially immerse ourselves in a threat simulation—a virtual world of danger. Through our engagement with characters in peril, we respond cognitively, emotionally, and physically to the horrors of the virtual world. The horror movie, then, is like a piece of software that runs on biological hardware. This hardware, the fear system, evolved to protect us from danger.[19]

The fear system, which is evolutionarily ancient, is tripwired to activate at the slightest cue of danger.[20] Imagine that you are home

Figure 1.3 You expect a horror movie to scare you, and horror movie ad campaigns often emphasize the scariness of a movie as a selling point. Some directors and producers will go to great lengths to promise potential audiences a real scare. The American filmmaker William Castle—king of the horror movie gimmick—took out life insurance for anybody who bought a ticket to his 1958 horror movie *Macabre* (Allied Artists), in case they should die of fright.

alone and hear a strange creaking noise from somewhere in the house. Your fear system is going to kick into action within a split second, setting off a cascade of psychological and physiological changes. Your body and mind, in short, get ready for attack. The heart beats faster to get a quick flow of blood to the big muscles. Your attention is sharply focused on the strange noise. You scan the surroundings, maybe looking for escape routes or something that could be used as a weapon. Within a few seconds, you are ready for flight or fight . . . and then it turns out to be the damned cat knocking something onto the floor, or a fridge compressor kicking in. But maybe, just maybe, that strange noise signals real danger—and if so, the fear response is useful.

Horror movies exploit this system. How do we know? Well, for one thing, consider the way people behave when they watch a horror movie. They show physiological and behavioral signs of fear. They are often anxious after the movie and sometimes have nightmares. All of that suggests that horror movies exploit the fear system. Additionally, recent neuroscientific evidence supports the hypothesis. In one study, a team of researchers recruited test subjects and put them into a brain scanner. They then showed the subject a horror movie—either *Insidious* or *Conjuring 2*—and measured brain activity. It turns out that scenes of creeping dread cause activity in brain regions associated with visual and auditory perception, whereas scenes of acute threat (also known as jump scares) cause activity in regions associated with threat evaluation and emotion processing.[21] The classic horror-movie buildup, it seems, causes viewers to increase vigilance, leading up to the jump scare that produces an all-out fight-or-flight response.

So when we are immersed in a horror movie, we are simulating a threat scenario. As other research has suggested, people are "designed" (by natural selection) to find simulation pleasurable because it is biologically adaptive, just like we find other adaptive behaviors pleasurable—having sex, say, or eating, or bonding with friends.[22] Through our engagement with fiction, we have exciting vicarious experiences that expand our horizons, and we learn about the world, especially the social world.[23] In horror specifically, we learn about the extremes of experience—vicariously, through the depiction of characters facing terror and shock, and personally, through experiencing extreme emotion ourselves.

Even if horror movies can be a force for good, lots of people are evidently very nervous about them. We will now look more closely at the various reasons people have for such nervousness, and we will begin by looking at one of the most notorious aspects of horror cinema—the jump scare. What is a jump scare, how does it work, and how can you protect yourself against it?

2

"I'm Nervous about the Jump Scares"

People who do not watch horror films often point to the "jump scare" as the main reason for their avoidance of such films. By jump scare, I mean the massive shock effect that often provides the climax for dread-drenched horror scenes. You know, the monster popping out of the closet or the ghost making a screaming entrance. And I get it, I do. Jump scares can be intensely unpleasant, and it is almost impossible to shield oneself against them. The jump scare is a cinematic grenade that the horror film lobs right into the nexus of your central nervous system. Sometimes it goes off before you even know what hit you. Other times it lies there for several seconds before exploding, and all you can do is stare at it anxiously, waiting for it to blow. Jump scares have a bad reputation, probably because they seem too primitive and easy to pull off, but they can be quite artful. And the biology and psychology behind the jump scare are fascinating.

Let me give an example of a particularly effective jump scare. This is one that had me literally jumping in the seat and gasping for breath. So I am watching the Netflix show *The Haunting of Hill House* with my family. The show, which is an adaptation of Shirley Jackson's classic horror novel, is about a haunted and dysfunctional family consisting of dad, mom (now dead), and four children: Nell, Luke, Theo, and Shirley. The show crosscuts between their childhood and adulthood. Grown-up Nell killed herself and is now haunting the others.

We are about half an hour into the episode—a particularly creepy one that has all of us on edge. Theo and Shirley are in a car, on their way to Hill House because they suspect Luke of being headed back to their dangerously haunted childhood home. The estranged sisters are engaged in a heated argument, filmed from within the dark car. Only their pale, emotional faces stand out on the screen—Theo to the left and Shirley to the right. There is darkness between them. The only sound, apart from their shouting match, is the faint noise of the car in the background. Suddenly, a face bursts from the darkness between the sisters and shoots toward the windshield. The movement is unnaturally swift. It is dead Nell, screaming violently and eerily, pale, with dead white eyes and black veins standing out in her cheeks and a wide-open mouth exposing rotted teeth (Fig. 2.1). The two living sisters are shocked and drive off the road.

When dead Nell burst into the dark space between the two sisters, my whole family jumped. I had been deeply engrossed in the episode, but now it was like my entire being resonated with that horrifying moment. My body galvanized itself with a real jolt, like an electrical shock, that seemed to radiate from my center to the extremities,

Figure 2.1 An exceptionally nasty jump scare occurs in the Netflix series *The Haunting of Hill House* (created by Mike Flanagan, 2018), in the episode "Witness Marks." Here two sisters are driving toward the place where the third sister committed suicide. They're arguing in the car when, suddenly, their dead sister pops up between them and screams violently. Man, that scene almost killed me.

producing a brief but intense pain in my hands and feet. The sensation was slightly unreal, like a momentary rupture in the fabric of things. I mean, I have been exposed to hundreds, if not thousands, of jump scares, but this one really caught me off guard and had me panting afterward, like I had been in a brush with death. But I also could not help but appreciate the artistry, the sheer craftsmanship, of a scene—a particular arrangement of visual and auditory stimuli emanating from a gadget in my living room—that had such an astounding effect. So, how and why does the horror film jump scare work? And is there anything you can do to avoid being knocked out of your skin by it?

Anatomy of the Jump Scare

The jump scare, which is also called the "film startle" and the "cinematic shock,"[1] has a long history in the film medium and beyond.[2] A jump scare occurs when a sudden and intense stimulus produces a so-called *startle response*. The precursor of the horror film jump scare can be found in the kind of playful behavior where somebody jumps up behind somebody else and yells "BOO!" (When scientists with an interest in the startle response scare the crap out of test subjects in the lab, they call it "administering a startle probe," which despite the clinical neutrality has a kind of sly, sadistic ring to it.) Such behavior, playfully startling others, probably goes back thousands of years, as a favorite pastime for our evolutionary ancestors—and as a crucial element in suspenseful oral storytelling. You can imagine a Paleolithic orator entertaining their audience with a thrilling tale of monster slayage or some such, peppering their verbal enactment of the tale with sound effects for dramatic effect. "He snuck into the monster's dark lair, hand axe at the ready. The reek of the monster was almost overpowering. He turned a corner, squinting in the darkness, and . . . ROAR, there was the monster, right in front of him!" For an engrossed and immersed audience, such an auditory gimmick would be an effective jump scare—a startle probe well administered.

The film scholar and jump scare expert Robert Baird notes that we can trace the cinematic jump scare back to the earliest days of film, for example with such allegedly startling cinematic experiences as the Lumière brothers' 1895 depiction of a train moving toward the audience. But Baird points to Val Lewton, the producer of the 1942 film *Cat People*, as the one who "formalized, even institutionalized, the startle for horror and thriller film."[3]

Cat People is about a Serbian woman, Irena Dubrovna, who claims that she transforms into a panther when she is in the throes of passion. She is in a relationship with one Oliver Reed, who is skeptical of her claim. He tells his assistant, Alice, about it. Irena finds out that Alice has a crush on Oliver and follows her home from a distance. In this famous scene, Alice is nervously running away from her unseen stalker. She reaches a bus stop. Suddenly, a loud hissing noise tears through the soundscape. As it turns out, the noise comes from an arriving bus, not a homicidal were-panther. Alice boards the bus to safety. This particular jump scare became known as a "bus"—a scene of dread that concludes with a startle that turns out to have been a false alarm.

The basic structure of a cinematic jump scare, according to Robert Baird, includes a character, an implied off-screen threat, and a "disturbing intrusion into the character's immediate space."[4] That is how it usually works, but there are variations—such as my example from *Haunting of Hill House*. Here the audience is completely unprepared for Nellie's intrusion. It is an incredibly tense scene because of the argument between the two characters and the sense that very bad things can happen at any moment, but the show has given us no reason to believe that the ghost is in the car. So that particular off-screen threat is not even implied. Typically, though, a dread-drenched scene leads up to an intense jump scare. The jump scare does not just come out of the blue. That is because the startle response can be primed like the carburetor in a lawnmower. If people are anxious, they respond to sudden stimuli with greater startle than if they are calm, because they already have anxiety juice in their mental carburetor.[5] And psychologists have shown that if you startle people who are looking at pictures of "mutilated bodies or spiders," they will startle more violently than if they are looking at pictures of "smiling children or nudes of the opposite sex."[6] The same principle is at work when a dreadful movie scene leads up to a startling climax. You are putting viewers in a jumpy state of mind to provoke an even stronger startle.

Sound is crucial to the jump scare. It is responsible for the better part of the startle, and it is almost impossible to counteract. An auditory stimulus can be processed faster than a visual one, and it takes more time to disrupt an auditory stimulus than it takes to disrupt a visual one. You can close your eyes or look away from a nasty image. You cannot close your ears or listen away.[7] Sound plays a crucial role in both parts of a scene that end with a jump scare—in both the buildup and the climax. In the buildup, the horror film uses sound, or the absence of sound, to establish an atmosphere of dread or apprehension. If there is sound in the buildup, it is often nondiegetic, which means that the sound is external to the filmic universe. The characters cannot hear it. That kind of sound can be mood music, such as the famous *duh-dun* motif of *Jaws*. It tells you that danger is approaching; it is basically a cue for you to get anxious. The sound can also be—and often is—acousmatic, which means that you hear the sound but you do not see what is causing it, which can be tremendously anxiety-provoking because it taps into a fear of the unknown.

Sometimes, however, a horror film will use silence to build up to the jump scare. Silence can be intensely unsettling in a horror film, and avid horror film watchers will know that silence is almost never good news. The absence of sound foreshadows something horrible. It is as if the horror movie is holding its breath. The horror fans know this, on a gut level, and their system goes into vigilance mode. Also, the sheer difference in signal strength between silence and startling sound actually works to increase the effect of the stimulus.[8]

The sonic buildup—whether consisting of unsettling mood music, silence, or sound effects—climaxes in an acoustic startle effect, also known as a "sound bump" or an "acoustic blast."[9] It is usually very loud diegetic sound, often mixed with equally loud nondiegetic sound—a scream, for instance, mixed with a boom or a so-called stinger (a sudden high-pitched sound). Consider the screaming violins that blend with Marion Crane's death screams in the infamous shower scene in Hitchcock's *Psycho*. Such sounds—screams, roars—target an ancient defensive mechanism in a fear system that humans share with many other species,[10] and they are incredibly effective in eliciting a powerful startle. They are like echoes from a distant past when a scream or a roar might mean immediate and mortal threat to our evolutionary ancestors. Such sounds certainly worked well in the scene from *Haunting of Hill House*, where Nell's scream blends with a low-pitched booming noise, possibly a roar, and what sounds like several other screams in a cacophony of horror.

The jump scare usually has a visual as well as an auditory element—something nasty that suddenly enters the frame. It is the sound that really makes viewers jump, but it is the visual element that tends to stick with them. You do not really remember the sound of a jump scare, but the imagery has the power to burn itself into your memory. The brain processes sound and images differently, and images are more easily remembered than sounds.[11] Typically, the visual part of the jump scare is a monster or a killer or something really disgusting suddenly entering the frame. Consider one of film history's most famous jump scares—the scene in *Jaws* where shark specialist Matt Hooper is scuba-diving, examining the wreck of a sunken boat with a bulky underwater flashlight. He is investigating a big hole in the hull of the boat and discovers a huge shark tooth lodged in the ragged edge of the hole. Eerie music is playing in the background. Suddenly, a severed, bloated head floats out of the hole, accompanied by a stinger and a scream. That bloated head, with pale wormlike creatures squirming in an otherwise empty eye socket, is not something you forget straightaway. It elicits a combination of disgust and fear in viewers: disgust because it is clearly decomposing, and our species has an evolved aversion toward decomposing flesh, especially when it is human flesh; and fear because it suggests predation. We realize that this is the work of the shark, and the shark could be nearby.

So, to startle viewers, the effective jump scare combines sound and image in a sequence of buildup leading to a shocking climax. Often the jump scare involves a character that we care about. In the scene from *Jaws*, Spielberg is careful to allow the viewer to empathize with poor Hooper as he discovers that creepy head. The result is that we respond not just to the nasty image and the startling sound, but also feel horror on behalf of Hooper. Spielberg uses a combination of point-of-view and reaction shots to get at this effect. We see Hooper discovering and investigating the hole. Hooper is in the right side of the frame, and the head floats out of the hole to the left. We then cut to a shot of Hooper's face, giving us a reaction shot. Hooper is startled. Then we get a point-of-view shot, focusing on that damnable head in a close-up. We see what Hooper sees. Cut to another reaction shot, showing Hooper panicking. When we share Hooper's perspective, both visually and emotionally, it is very hard not to feel an echo of his horror.

This whole sequence expertly uses the affordances of the film medium to manipulate us, from low-level physiological stimulation to more sophisticated cognitive and emotional manipulation. Don't let anybody tell you that a horror movie jump scare is stupid and easy. It can be, yes, but it can also be a surprisingly complex artistic device and a crucial element in a film designed to disturb and unsettle you. The startle response may look like a pretty primitive reflex, the operation of which can be reduced to a simple formula: BOO → AAAH! But it is actually a quite sophisticated, context-sensitive adaptation that has kept organisms alive for millions of years, and it can be exploited in artful ways by horror films.

The Startle Response

The jump scare produces a so-called startle response, and the startle response is hardwired into human nature. It is so biologically fundamental that we share it with many other species. Indeed, startle is "universal in mammals, reptiles, birds, and amphibians,"[12] according to the anthropologist and startle expert Ronald C. Simons. It is an "invariant response" to a "sudden, intense stimulus."[13] That stimulus can be visual, auditory, or tactile.[14] It can be something that suddenly pops up in your visual field, a sudden noise, or something touching the back of your neck when you thought you were alone in a dark basement. The startle response evolved to protect us from sudden danger, and it works by rapidly galvanizing the organism in the face of threat.[15] The startle process was described by two scientists, Landis and Hunt, in a classical study from 1932, as involving

> blinking of the eyes, head movement forward, a characteristic facial expression, raising and drawing forward of the shoulders, abduction of the upper arms, bending of the elbows, pronation of the lower arms, flexion of the fingers, forward movement of the trunk, contraction of the abdomen, and bending of the knees.[16]

The purpose of the whole sequence, which typically takes about a second or less, is to protect vital organs and make the organism ready for confrontation with a threat. The eye-blink, which occurs as swiftly as 30–50 milliseconds after the startling stimulus,[17] protects the eyes from trauma. It is followed by a widening of the eyes, which enlarges the visual field to allow for better threat assessment. The eyebrows shoot up to help open the eyes faster and wider. The mouth opens in a surprised O, probably to allow for a rapid intake of breath in anticipation of exertion. There is an almost-instantaneous up-regulation of the sympathetic nervous system, which is the branch of our autonomic nervous system that is responsible for the fight-or-flight response. Adrenaline and noradrenaline are released into the bloodstream, increasing heart rate and sweat secretion. The startle response is, in essence, an adaptive mechanism that prepares your system for action and tells you: *Heads the fuck up!* (Apologies for the vulgarity, but it only seems appropriate: Scientists have shown that startled people frequently resort to inappropriate language, such as "coprolalia"—dung-talk—or terms that refer to "sexual anatomy or activity.")[18]

The psychologist Silvan Tomkins describes the startle response as an "interrupter mechanism" and compares it with those traffic announcements that a car radio sometimes sends out to interrupt the ongoing broadcast with information about a traffic jam or road construction work or some such.[19] The startle response is like that.

You are walking along a path in the forest, lost in thoughts, when a nearby screech jolts you. Your body goes through the process just described, and you forget all about your ruminations. The whole system is in a split second oriented to what could be a threat. If the screech turns out to be a pouncing predator, great, you are ready to run and your viscera may get to stay inside your body. If it is just a harmless bird crying out, no worries. You got a scare, that's all. Maybe the bird did too. Back to walking and thinking. Your physiological and attentional settings can go back to where they were before that nasty sound.

It is very easy to elicit a startle in others because the mechanism is on a hair trigger, and for good evolutionary reasons. It is like the emotion of fear, which also tends to overshoot—simply because a false positive (jumping at shadows) is better than a false negative (shrugging at a cue that turns out to be lethal). Also, the startle response is cognitively impenetrable.[20] You cannot switch it off, and there is little you can do to attenuate the response even if you know a startle is coming. Anybody who has fired a big gun knows this is true. And anybody who has seen the same horror film twice and jumped at the same scare knows it too.

Surviving the Jump Scare

The startle response provoked by the jump scare can be unpleasant. The rapid and massive activation of skeletal muscles can even be a little painful, like receiving a mild electrical shock. People differ in the degree to which they startle. Some people are "hyperstartlers," some are exceedingly difficult to startle, and most people are somewhere in between those extremes.[21] People also differ in the degree to which they enjoy intense physiological arousal. So-called thrill seekers tend to enjoy it.[22] But if you are not a thrill seeker and not a big fan of being startled by a jump scare, what can you do?

It is difficult to avoid jump scares without also avoiding horror films, but there are horror films with no jump scares. *The Blair Witch Project* is one. Apparently, though, the jump scare is more frequent in horror films than it used to be. Baird chalks it down to "the hypersensationalization of the post-*Psycho* horror/thriller film."[23] Whatever the reason, the website wheresthejump.com delivers statistics on jump scare frequency in about 250 movies.[24] A typical present-day horror film has an average of 10 jump scares. Compare that to a horror film from the 1960s, which had only, on average, 2.6 jump scares. That number increased to 5.6 in the 1970s and then almost doubled in the 1980s, with an average of 9.5 jump scares per horror film (probably because of the prevalence of startle-happy slasher films in that decade). The number dropped in the 1990s, but seems now to be settling at an average of 10 per film. Perhaps that is a natural optimum for the frequency of jump scares per horror film—a frequency that optimally stimulates viewers' fear system and startle response without exhausting them. Too many startles can lead to habituation (they lose their potency), whereas just enough startles can lead to sensitization—one startle primes you for the next startle, which is felt more strongly and which primes you for the next startle, and so on.

If you cannot easily avoid jump scares without also avoiding horror films, you can try to reduce the effect of the startle. Do not watch a horror film if you are very tired, because your fear system is more responsive when you are sleep-deprived,[25] and your startle response is likely to be more active than otherwise. Same if you are feeling anxious or jumpy.[26] It is also more difficult to regulate your emotions when you are worn out.[27] So look inside yourself before watching a horror film, and ask yourself if you might be better off postponing it. Also, there is some evidence that the startle response can be muted with the aid of, ah, chemistry, but I don't recommend that. Alcohol, however, is known to reduce the magnitude of startle,[28] so you might consider having a beer or a glass of wine before the film.

Additionally, if it is the jump scare that you are really nervous about, do not watch horror films in the cinema. Modern movie theaters are designed for maximum immersion and minimal distraction. They have awesome sound systems, and we have seen how important sound is to the jump scare. Moreover, a movie theater is dark, and psychologists have demonstrated in the lab that people startle more violently in dark than in light surroundings.[29] At home, you can switch on the lights. And if you do watch horror films at home and have a good sound system with surround, consider switching the surround system off. Surround leads to increased immersion, which leads to enhancement of emotional response—including the startle response.[30] Turn down the volume. Doing so will decrease the effect of the jump scare. It will not protect you from those nasty images, but there is a difference between seeing a nasty image on a 40-inch screen in your living room and seeing it on a cinema screen that is 40 by 30 *feet*.

You can also become a horror movie expert and learn to decode and predict such films. I have seen a lot of horror films, and I can usually tell when a jump scare is on the horizon—from the soundscape, the pattern of editing, plot progression, and so on. The thing is, horror movie directors know that horror buffs are good at predicting jump scares, so horror directors will try to cheat the buffs by manipulating the jump scare formula. They may, for example, lead up to what appears to be a jump scare but turns out to be a false alarm—only to then, when the viewer is relieved and relaxed, turn on the horror jets, full force.[31] There is a scene in *IT: Chapter One* from 2017 where one of the child characters, Beverly, is chased by her crazy dad but manages to take him out in the bathroom. Whew, she got away from that maniac. She turns and then, BAM, there's the killer clown. Nobody saw that coming (unless they visited wheresthejump.com before watching the film).

So, learning the conventions and the patterns of horror films may help you a bit, but it will not completely protect you from the jump scare. If you do know it is coming, though, you can employ coping strategies in an attempt to keep your fear response on a leash. At the very least, you can reduce the pre-startle anxiety, which may attenuate the startle itself. Effective coping strategies include self-distraction (think about something else) and reframing (try to remind yourself that it is just a movie).[32] Behavioral interventions such as looking away or covering your eyes have limited immediate effect because they do not block the sound—but they do block the images. So there could be a long-term benefit, since it is the images that stick with you, as we have seen. Moreover, so-called antecedent coping strategies—which are employed *before* the frightening stimulus hits you—are more effective than response-oriented coping strategies for fear regulation. It is more effective to nip a fear response in the bud than to beat it into the ground once it has sprouted. That is because the fear response is pretty resistant to cognitive, rational control. Once it gets going, there is very little you can do. The startle response, however, is even more resistant. So even the use of antecedent coping strategies may be fairly ineffective.

My own favorite coping strategy for jump scares is to try to adopt an aesthetic, appreciative perspective. I try to see the jump scare as an aesthetic technique. If you approach a horror film from that perspective, you will find that you are less immersed.[33] It does not always work, and it certainly does not work when the jump scare happens. In the very moment of the jump scare I am reduced to primitive biology—to primate grunts, dancing limbs, and fizzing nerve endings. But immediately afterward, I try to see how the jump scare was constructed. Doing so gives me a bit of psychological distance from the stimulus that just gutted me and allows me to appreciate the artistry of it. You can do the same—but do it at home, with the sound turned down and the lights turned on and perhaps a bit of alcohol in your blood.

Box 2.1 Three Horror Films to Watch If You're Nervous about Jump Scares

- *Rosemary's Baby* by Roman Polanski (1969). This horror classic about a demonic pregnancy relies on suspense and psychological terror rather than in-your-face effects such as gore, monsters, and jump scares—and it's incredibly tense even after all these years. Recommended fare for the jump-scare weary.
- *Session 9* by Brad Anderson (2001). This relatively overlooked horror thriller about a renovation crew getting into serious trouble in an old asylum is heavy on atmosphere and dread and has not a single jump scare.
- *Bone Tomahawk* by S. Craig Zahler (2015). This genre-bending horror Western—Zahler's first feature film—was produced on a tiny budget and features a rescue team venturing into desolate lands inhabited by creepy cannibals. Plenty of atmosphere and delightful dialogue; no jump scares.

Box 2.2 Three Horror Films *Not* to Watch If You're Nervous about Jump Scares

- *The Woman in Black* by James Watkins (2012). It's an excellent and deeply disturbing film, but it's got a high jump-scare count. There's a particularly nasty one involving the protagonist, a ghost, and a window. Thinking about the scene still gives me goosebumps.
- *The Conjuring* by James Wan (2013). Avoid this screamer if you're not into jump scares—there are some *really* bad ones about 40 minutes into the movie. Well, avoid the entire *Conjuring* franchise—including the spin-offs featuring Annabelle the Possessed and Ultra-Evil Doll.
- *IT* by Andy Muschietti (2017). Also a good horror film, but it has 23 jump scares, according to wheresthejump.com—18 minor ones and five major ones. And a couple of those major ones will make you jump out of your skin.

3

"I'm Nervous about Horror Films and My Mental Health"

On December 26, 1973, the horror film *The Exorcist* hit American movie theaters. The film was based on a well-known and notoriously scary bestseller from 1971—William Peter Blatty's *The Exorcist*, which was supposedly based on an actual 1949 possession case in the United States. When the film opened after a long and fairly troubled production, hype had been building steadily. Rumors had been circulating that the movie was cursed. A set burned down, several crew and cast members died, and various tragedies struck others involved with the film. The director, William Friedkin, shrewdly played along with these rumors in interviews, but of course any number of mishaps are apt to strike a huge film production that stretches out over a whole year.[1] Even so, by the time the film premiered, people were flocking to see what the fuss was about (Fig. 3.1). In cold New York City, patrons were waiting in lines that stretched for several city blocks. Could it really be true that this film, about a young girl possessed by a demon, was *that* scary?

Yes. The film was exceptionally scary. A reporter writing for the *New York Times* described the movie's reception a month after its release. She wrote:

> It's been reported that once inside the theater, a number of moviegoers vomited at the very graphic goings-on on the screen. Others fainted, or left the theater, nauseous and trembling, before the film was half over. Several people had heart attacks, a guard told me. One woman even had a miscarriage, he said.[2]

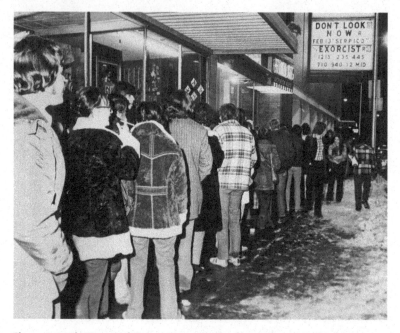

Figure 3.1 *The Exorcist* (Warner Bros., directed by William Friedkin) drew enormous crowds when it opened in movie theaters just after Christmas of 1973. Here, people are standing in the freezing cold, waiting to see if the already-notorious film is really that scary. SuperStock/Alamy Stock Photo.

The press carried many such reports. *Time* magazine had a February 1974 feature on what it called "Exorcist Fever." The reporter had spoken to *Exorcist* patrons, movie theater operators, psychiatrists, and religious clergy, and claimed that some moviegoers were so harrowed by what they had seen in *The Exorcist* that they went to seek spiritual or even psychiatric treatment.[3]

If you are worried that horror films will mess you up, the extraordinary reception of *The Exorcist* probably will not put your worries to rest. Don't swear off horror movies just yet, though. People are very seldom seriously damaged psychologically by horror movies. There are some documented cases of PTSD-like symptoms resulting from horror, but in such cases, other factors are usually at play.

A 1975 scientific article in the *Journal of Nervous and Mental Disease* set out to investigate the reports of neurosis and psychosis allegedly caused by *The Exorcist*.[4] The author, a medical doctor, described four cases of what he called "cinematic neurosis." One case involved a young man who had been taken to the emergency room by his father, who in the dead of night had found his son awake in bed, "clutching a Bible in the dark," after the young man had seen *The Exorcist*. He was unable to sleep for several nights, was afraid he might become possessed by the Devil and punished for past wrongdoings, and took to drink and drugs in an attempt to get the nasty scenes from the film out of his head. The other three cases were similar. The thing is, though, all four individuals had serious problems in their lives before they went to see *The Exorcist*.

A later study, published in 2007, went over the scientific literature and found only seven documented cases of cinematic neurosis— five cases related to *The Exorcist*, one to *Jaws*, and one to *Invasion of the Body Snatchers*.[5] The authors of the study said that cinematic neurosis is a syndrome "whereby a film shapes the symptom presentation of pre-existing mental health conditions in vulnerable people."[6] In other words, a horror film may stimulate and give shape to existing psychological problems in certain individuals. Other researchers have pointed to serious but isolated cases of trauma-like responses to a British pseudo-documentary television show called *Ghostwatch*.[7]

Ghostwatch was shown on BBC on Halloween night in 1992 and depicted reporters setting out to investigate an allegedly haunted house, where they found frightening evidence of poltergeist activity. The show was made to look like a live documentary broadcast with shaky handheld cameras and technical glitches and everything (Fig. 3.2), but it was all staged and filmed in advance and scripted by the Welsh horror writer Stephen Volk. Thousands of shocked viewers called up the BBC to complain about the show, jamming the switchboard.

A mentally disabled man, 18-year-old Martin Denham, watched *Ghostwatch* with his parents and became obsessed with thoughts of

Figure 3.2 The British pseudo-documentary *Ghostwatch* (created by Stephen Volk and directed by Leslie Manning) was broadcast on the BBC in 1992 . . . and never again shown on British television. The show, which appeared to provide live coverage of an actual poltergeist, caused tens of thousands of upset viewers to call the BBC, jamming their switchboard. In this image from the movie, well-known BBC host Michael Parkinson and a paranormal expert, Dr. Lin Pascoe (Gillian Bevan), discuss what appears to be surveillance footage of the poltergeist.

ghosts. He killed himself five days later, leaving a note for his mother in which he said: "If there is ghosts I will now be one and I will always be with you as one."[8] Two 10-year-old boys saw the show and developed PTSD-like symptoms, such as panic attacks, intrusive thoughts of ghosts and images from the show, and serious sleep disorders, and were referred to a child psychiatry unit, where they received treatment.[9] Both boys recovered, and while *Ghostwatch* seems to have set off their disorders, their doctors noted that both boys had "anxiety traits and overdependent relationships." BBC disowned the show and issued a public apology.

So while isolated cases of lasting negative effects of exposure to horror media exist, full-blown cinematic neurosis is very rare. For the vast majority of people, horror films pose no threat to their sanity.

Lingering Fright Reactions

What about milder forms of psychological distress? Is it not possible that a horror film will ruin your sleep for a night or two, compel you to do a monster sweep of the bedroom before you turn in, and fill your head with nasty images that are difficult or even impossible to get rid of?

Yes. Media researchers have since the 1980s been busy analyzing what they tend to call "lingering fright reactions" to scary films and television.[10] Most of that research focuses on children—a topic we are saving for a later chapter—but there are also studies of lingering fright in adolescents and grown-ups. Those studies point in the same direction: Lingering fright from exposure to horror—expressed as mild behavioral and sleep disturbances—is very common. Lots of folks have had nightmares because of horror films, or slept with the lights on, or avoided certain situations, such as swimming in the sea after watching *Jaws* or going camping after watching *The Blair Witch Project*.

One study, published in 1989, surveyed a group of American college students, asking about their memories of lingering fright in response to horror. Almost half of the sample said that they often felt nervous after watching a horror movie. A similar proportion said that they "sometimes experienced trouble getting to sleep after watching a scary show or movie."[11] Another study, also asking American college students about their experiences, found that 90% of the sample had experienced lingering fright reactions. Half of those said they had experienced "disturbances in normal behavior such as sleeping or eating," and about a third "avoided or dreaded the depicted situation."[12]

One of the leading experts on the subject, the media researcher Joanne Cantor, published a study in which she asked her students to write short papers about mass media that had frightened them at some point in their lives. The data for the study was collected in the years 1997–2000, and she got reports from 530 students, most of whom had stories to tell about lingering fright reactions to horror movies. The four most frequently mentioned films in this sample were *Poltergeist*, *Jaws*, *The Blair Witch Project*, and *Scream*.

Intriguingly, those films affected Cantor's students slightly differently. Certain films were much more likely than others to have caused "bedtime problems," for example, by which Cantor means nightmares, sleeplessness, or what she calls "specific 'protective behaviors' in bed"[13]—presumably referring to such time-honored monster protection strategies as ensuring that no limbs protrude from underneath the covers. Among the 29 students who mentioned *Poltergeist* as a film that had produced lingering fright reactions in them, 72% mentioned bedtime problems as a symptom. Only 18% of the 22 students who mentioned *The Blair Witch Project* said that the film had produced sleep disturbances. Evidently, the horror of *Poltergeist*—a supernatural horror movie about malevolent ghosts who abduct a girl to a metaphysical dimension—provides better fuel for nighttime fears. Most of the horror scenes in *Poltergeist* play out in the protagonists' home, or even in a bedroom. Not that *The Blair Witch Project* didn't mess people up, though. Of the ones who had been frightened by *Blair Witch*—a horror film about three youngsters who get lost in the woods and end up dead—73% said that the film had had "effects on waking life," such as causing viewers to avoid camping trips or recreational walks in the woods.

Women seem to be more susceptible than men to the lingering effects identified by Cantor and her colleagues.[14] In one study, 57% of female respondents said they "often feel nervous" after watching a scary film. Only 27% of male respondents said that.[15] It could be that women on average are more willing to admit that a horror film has messed them up, just as they are more likely to use physical, so-called *behavioral* coping strategies when a horror film frightens them badly. They cover their eyes or look away. Men, in contrast, tend to prefer invisible, cognitive strategies, such as attempts at self-distraction. The standard explanation for these findings is that it is perfectly socially acceptable for women to display fear, whereas men are expected to show mastery.[16] But as I mentioned in the introduction, both biological and social factors seem to be at play.

The kinds of lingering fright reactions I have just discussed—mild sleep disturbances, temporarily increased vigilance, and so on—may be unpleasant, but they are perfectly natural. Horror movies are designed to jump-start the fear system, and once that system gets going, it is difficult to switch it off again. There is a little scout deep inside your brain who has been roused and is now looking frantically for danger, and he does not stop looking just because the movie is over. His job is to keep you alive. If making you double-check under the bed increases the odds, ever so slightly, of you making it through the night, well, then that is what he does.

So, the prevalence of lingering fright reactions should not worry you too much. As the psychology professor G. Neil Martin concluded in a huge 2019 study that fine-combed decades of horror media effects research, "There is no evidence that exposure to horror films has adverse or sustained effects on mental health in individuals with no pre-existing mental health issue."[17] But horror movies can still have spillover effects, for example by showing you something that you cannot "unsee," as the kids say, or by conveying an idea that unsettles you.

The Power of Nasty Images

Let us return, for a moment, to *The Exorcist*. Why did that film disturb viewers so powerfully? The story it tells is pretty simple. A young girl, Regan, starts behaving strangely, with violent outbursts and sleep disturbances. Her mom, Chris, seeks psychiatric help, but the doctors are stumped. Regan's condition deteriorates rapidly. She becomes increasingly violent and diseased-looking. Chris eventually turns to the clergy, recruiting a couple of Jesuit priests who end up determining demonic possession as the cause of Regan's problems. The demon is eventually exorcised and Regan saved.

A simple story . . . but there is something about the way it is told, and the ideas it conveys, that really made it an exceptionally shocking horror movie. As the film critic Roger Ebert wrote when it came out, *The Exorcist* "doesn't rest on the screen; it's a frontal assault."[18] The director, William Friedkin, deftly used state-of-the-art visual effects to create unforgettable images, such as possessed Regan spinning her head around. And the soundtrack alone—for which the film won an Academy Award—is deeply unsettling. The film's sound designer, Ron Nagle, recorded the sounds of angry bees and pigs being led to slaughter and mixed those sounds into the film's soundtrack. Ebert called the film "an exploitation of the most fearsome resources of cinema." It is true. Friedkin did mobilize all the most fearsome resources of cinema to elicit a symphony of negative emotions, ranging from primitive, unreflected startle and gross-out to superstitious terror and existential dread.

The film has several well-orchestrated jump scares, and we saw in the previous chapter how effective they can be. It also offers a generous dose of fear and disgust imagery, especially in the depiction of Regan in her advanced demon-infested state. She looks like she might be carrying a highly contagious disease (Fig. 3.3), and it is a powerful effect because humans are hardwired to respond with aversion to individuals who exhibit cues of infection.[19] Her extremely transgressive behavior, too, elicits disgust—but moral, rather than visceral, disgust. Take, for instance, the scene where the 12-year-old girl violates herself with a crucifix in front of her horrified mother, growling, "Let Jesus fuck you" in an eerily distorted, demonic voice. Visceral disgust evolved to protect us from disease; moral disgust evolved to protect the fabric of our social structures by mobilizing an aversive reaction toward norm violations, especially purity violations (such as the corruption of an innocent child).[20] Demonic Regan elicits both kinds of disgust.

There is one scene in particular that made viewers queasy, and that is where Regan is being subjected to a medical procedure known as a cerebral angiography. That procedure is used to visualize the blood vessels in the brain. A thin tube is inserted into a large artery in the neck and threaded to a carotid artery, and a chemical substance is

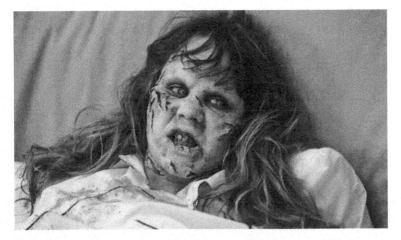

Figure 3.3 Demon-possessed Regan MacNeil (Linda Blair) looks like she might be carrying an infectious disease. Such disgust-evoking cues are frequent in horror movies because they powerfully tap into an ancient defense mechanism in human nature. Screenshot from *The Exorcist* (Warner Bros., directed by William Friedkin, 1973).

injected. When that substance spreads to the blood vessels in the brain, X-ray technology is used to take pictures of the patient's head. The procedure helps detect aneurysms and other circulatory malfunctions in the brain. Friedkin shows us the procedure in all its grisly horror, drawing on his experience as a documentary filmmaker to invest the scene, which was shot at New York University Medical Center, with disturbing authenticity.

Regan is wheeled into an examination room, where a couple of medical professionals prepare her for the procedure. We see (and hear) the needle go into Regan's neck in an extreme close-up. We see Regan grimace in pain and hear her whimper. We see the arterial blood pulsing from the needle and splash onto Regan's hospital gown until the catheter is inserted and threaded into an artery (Fig. 3.4). And we see the chemical substance, the contrast agent, being pumped into her. We hear the buzzing of the medical machines and the loud mechanical banging noises of the imaging equipment. The point of the scene is to emphasize the dangerous impotence of

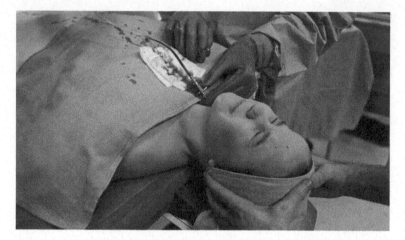

Figure 3.4   The infamous angiography scene from *The Exorcist* (Warner Bros., directed by William Friedkin, 1973). The scene, with its realistic and graphic depiction of a grisly medical procedure, powerfully taps into a common aversion toward blood and injury.

the medical establishment in the face of supernatural intervention, I guess, but it also works on a much more primitive level. I have seen that scene a dozen times and it still makes me squirm.

The angiography scene taps into a very common aversion toward blood and injury. In fact, there is a specific and fairly widespread phobia called "blood-injury-injection phobia." People suffering from this phobia—and that is about 3%–4% of the general population—tend to feel intense aversion at the sight or anticipation of blood, injury, injection, or even disability, and may faint when they are exposed to these stimuli. In fact, the fainting sets this particular phobia apart from other phobias. Arachnophobes do not faint at the sight of a spider; they get away from it as fast as possible. Their fight-or-flight response is triggered with a sharp increase in heart rate and blood pressure. That makes sense, from an evolutionary perspective. Steel the organism for confrontation or evasion. Get away from the eight-legged threat as fast as possible.

So why do blood-injury-injection phobics faint? Well, they also experience an increase in heart rate and blood pressure when they are exposed to phobic objects, but that increase is followed by a sudden decrease, which causes symptoms such as dizziness, nausea, and fainting.[21] It may sound like a glitch in the system, but this so-called biphasic response—the increase and then decrease in heart rate and blood pressure—is probably a design feature; an evolutionary adaptation. Fainting at the sight of blood or injury could be adaptive if you have hurt yourself, or been hurt by a predator. The decreased blood pressure prevents excessive hemorrhage, and if you are lying lifeless on the ground, the sabretooth tiger may decide to head off in search of more lively prey. That kind of playing-dead, or tonic immobility, is fairly common in the animal kingdom and probably evolved as a defensive strategy to avoid being eaten.

Even those of us who do not suffer from blood-injury-injection phobia may not feel so hot at the sight of a gaping wound or a dismembered corpse. The aversion we feel makes evolutionary sense. Body-envelope violations can be dangerous—to oneself, obviously, but also in others. An open wound is a portal for disease transmission, and a corpse is a hotbed for pathogens and so carries a real danger of infection.

Of course, our aversion toward body violations is in tension with a morbid curiosity about what is inside a body—the kind of curiosity that compels many people to watch CSI-type shows or listen to grisly true crime podcasts. Morbid curiosity too makes evolutionary sense. It pays, in the currency of survival, to find pleasure in learning about the Grim Reaper and his many tools and modes of operation.[22]

The behavioral scientist Coltan Scrivner has done pioneering work on the psychology of morbid curiosity. He has found that morbid curiosity is a personality trait that is normally distributed in the population. That means that a few people are extremely morbidly curious, a few people are not morbidly curious at all, and the rest of us—the majority—are somewhere between these two extremes. Moreover, Scrivner has found that morbid curiosity has four facets. The first facet, "motives of dangerous people," describes curiosity about the minds and motives of serial killers, for example. The second facet, "supernatural danger," is curiosity about subjects such as the occult and haunted places. The third facet, "social violence," is curiosity about what violence and homicide look like. The fourth facet, "body violation," is curiosity about surgery, autopsies, and so on. Intriguingly, it is possible to score highly on only some of these facets. A person may be intensely interested in motives of dangerous people and listen to true crime podcasts for recreation, say, and be a serial killer documentary buff, but be highly squeamish about CSI-type television shows and show no interest at all in the supernatural.[23] And perhaps unsurprisingly, Scrivner has found that people high in morbid curiosity are more likely to be horror fans than people low in morbid curiosity.[24]

Horror movies exploit our powerfully ambivalent feelings toward depictions of blood and injury. That stuff is nasty, but it is also fascinating, especially when it is safely packaged within a fiction film—when you can remind yourself that it is just special effects. The subgenre sometimes known as "splatter"—characterized by extensive and explicit depictions of mutilation, gore, and graphic violence—lives off this fascination.[25] (Tellingly, the 1963 movie that is commonly identified as the first splatter film is called *Blood Feast*.) So does the more recent phenomenon of "gorenography" or "torture porn," which also revels in explicit depictions of mutilation and violence. (We will revisit that subgenre in a later chapter, when we talk about horror movies and morality.) But even less gory fare tends to include some depiction of blood and injury. That stuff is powerful, especially if we are emotionally invested in the movie character who is being injured.[26]

If a film has encouraged us to establish an empathetic bond with a character and that character is injured, we mirror the pain of that injury more intensely than if it happens to a character that we do not care about. That kind of mirror affect is sometimes called "affective mimicry,"[27] and it happens automatically. The psychological mechanisms responsible for affective mimicry are hardwired into our brains and probably evolved to facilitate social interaction. It is important to be able to put yourself in other people's shoes, and to infer their inner state, when you are engaging with them—whether cooperatively or agonistically. Horror movies take advantage of this aspect of human nature when they depict bad things happening to good characters. The so-called reaction shot is a great tool for making viewers mirror the pain of movie characters. Take that angiography scene from *The Exorcist*. We do not just get close-ups of needles and blood, we also get facial shots of poor Regan and of her mother watching, anxiously, behind a glass plate (Fig. 3.5). Our revulsion at the bad things happening to Regan is strengthened if we feel empathy toward Regan and her mom, and we mirror their pain.

Sometimes horror movies show us things that we cannot forget. An image may lodge itself in our mind, maybe in time sinking into the bubbling tar pits of the subconscious but occasionally seeping back up into consciousness like a demonic, tar-dripping jack-in-the-box. When I go into our basement alone and it is dark outside, I often get these flashbulb-like inner visions of scenes from horror movies, such as a screaming face with empty black eyes or a pale woman with long black hair crawling out of a television set. Some things are more

Figure 3.5 Regan's mom, Chris MacNeil (Ellen Burstyn), looking on at her young daughter's angiography. The focus on her anxious facial expression invites viewers to share her emotional state, which is a common technique in horror movies. We see terrible and disgusting things, but we also adopt the perspective of characters responding to those terrible and disgusting things. Screenshot from *The Exorcist* (Warner Bros., directed by William Friedkin, 1973).

likely to stick in our memory than others, and the phenomenon of "adaptive memory" helps explain why.

The big idea among adaptive memory scientists is that memory systems evolved to retain information that is relevant for survival and reproduction, and they have collected a lot of empirical data to support this idea.[28] Basically, the human memory is biased to retain some kinds of information over other kinds. We are really good at remembering strategic social information—somebody being really nasty to you, for example, or committing some enormous violation of social norms. We are also really good at remembering information about danger. We are not so good at remembering the formula for calculating the volume of a sphere, say, or the Social Security number of a relative.

In ancestral times, when our ancestors lived as hunter-gatherers in dangerous natural and social environments, it paid to have vivid memories of dangers, and we modern humans retain our ancestors' adaptive biases for memory encoding and recall. Hunter-gatherers in the Pleistocene did not have to worry about exact spheric volume or Social Security numbers, but they needed to keep a mental record of who was nasty and who was nice, and they damn well had to pay attention to the hunting habits of feline predators and remember the exact location of a hidden crevice. So our attention is drawn by the horrible sights offered by horror movies, and the horrible sights are mnemonically "sticky," lodging themselves in our memory banks whether we want them to or not.[29]

Likewise, psychologists have found that urban legends are more likely to be passed on if they contain social information or emotionally arousing material.[30] Nobody would care about an urban legend about a schoolteacher forgetting the formula for spheric volume calculation. But an urban legend about razor blades in apples distributed to kids at Halloween, about spider nests in dreadlocks or alligators in sewer systems . . . that stuff rouses our interest. So do tales about somebody doing something wildly inappropriate to somebody else. We are innately curious about what other people are up to, which explains our undying appetite for gossip, and we are innately curious about threats in our environments.

I once gave a lecture on the psychology of horror movies to an audience of high school teachers. One of the teachers came up to me afterward. He had been puzzling over why he had vivid memories of horror B-movies he had seen as a teenager but could not remember the plot of a Paul Auster novel he had read the previous month. Well, part of the reason has to be that horror trades in images that hijack our attentional and mnemonic systems. The stylistic and philosophical pirouettes of a postmodern novel may tickle the intellect, but our Stone Age brains do not necessarily find questions of ontological and epistemological ambiguity very memorable. Frothing monsters and maniacs with roaring chainsaws, though? That stuff goes straight into the limbic brain and stays there. But sometimes horror movies are disturbing not just because of the things they show us—sometimes it is the ideas embedded in a horror movie that get us.

The Power of Terrifying Ideas

The power of *The Exorcist* cannot just be attributed to the nasty visceral stuff depicted in the film—the demonic faces, the projectile vomiting, and so on. As the reviewer for *Variety* wrote, back when the film came out: "The climactic sequences assault the senses and the intellect with pure cinematic terror."[31] That is exactly right: the senses *and* the intellect. What really troubled a lot of viewers was the conceptual, more so than the perceptual, material—the ideas conveyed by the film. Take the film's notion that absolute evil exists as a real force in the world, a force that can literally possess innocent people and make them do morally reprehensible things. That is not a nice idea, and the film presented this idea as reality; something that was true, at least within the film's world. The realism of the film—its documentary cinematography, contemporary setting, and the naturalistic performances of the actors—helped make that idea seem plausible. Here was an evil force infesting an all-American girl living in Georgetown, in Washington, DC, not some ancient crumbling castle in the Carpathian mountains. The film got a lot of people thinking, and not in a pleasant way.

Even for people who do not believe in anything spiritual or metaphysical, the notion of demonic possession is disturbing. We can entertain ideas even though we do not believe they are true—what-if scenarios. When we do so, we feel the emotional impact of those ideas and scenarios. Imagine biting into a sandwich and discovering a spider the size of a golf ball inside. I mean, really imagine it—close your eyes and get that scene in sharp focus in your mind's eye. Disgusting, right? It is not just an image in your mind, it is an image that comes with an emotional flavor (disgust). Kids engage in such "decoupled cognition," as psychologists call it, when they pretend-play. They know they are not really a dog or a superhero, but they can still simulate an imaginative world in which that is the case. They will be happy when the super-hero thwarts the bad guys' evil plans of overtaking the world or kidnapping the princess or whatever, and they will be sad when the pretend-dog is scolded by its pretend-owner for taking a pretend-leak on the pretend-carpet. They will be frightened by the pretend-monster chasing them. That is one of the primary functions of imagination—to run simulations of the world, and to register their emotional valence.[32] A world simulation infested with supernatural forces of darkness is frightening whether you believe in such forces or not. But of course, if you do believe in the supernatural, you are likely to be more affected by movies depicting supernatural evil.[33] Such movies will evoke and confirm your worst fear.

Horror films can also disturb us by sensitizing us to ideas that are less implausible than demonic possession. If you are a bit of a wor-rier, prone to worst-case thinking, and are familiar with the films in the *Final Destination* series, you will know exactly what I am talking about. In this delightfully irreverent and creative franchise, young people are hunted down by the Grim Reaper. One character has a precognitive vision of impending doom and changes the course of destiny by avoiding the deaths of himself and his friends. Death is now trying to set things right by sequentially killing off the kids in increasingly innovative freak accidents, which involve not monsters or demonic forces but everyday objects.

In *Final Destination* 3, for example, a pair of young women enter a tanning salon. The audience knows that Death is waiting for them, but not how he will take care of them. One of the women carelessly places a half-empty cup of slush ice above an electronic device that regulates the wattage of the ultraviolet tanning lamps. She slides into place in the tanning bed. Condensation from the cup begins to drip into the device, causing a short-circuit that has the effect of amping up the power of the tanning lamps. The rising heat causes the AC to kick in. The airstream from the vent blows over a coat tree that knocks over a plant that hits a loosely fitted shelf that falls onto the tanning beds, effectively pinning the women within (Fig. 3.6) while the temperature and UV light intensity keep going up. You can imagine the rest. It is not pretty. The *Final Destination* films are full of such uncanny causal sequences that may be improbable in the real world, but that are all too disturbingly familiar to the worriers among us. *What if* . . .

Characters in horror films are seldom safe because safety is not scary. They are hunted and assaulted and mangled and killed. Films in the so-called body horror subgenre, which is characterized by excesses of mutilations and bodily transformations,[34] tend to

Figure 3.6 The inventive film series *Final Destination* exploits a natural human tendency for worst-case thinking. In *Final Destination* 3 (New Line Cinema, directed by James Wong, 2006), two young women are trapped inside their tanning beds as the temperature reaches lethal levels because of a series of freak accidents.

focus excruciatingly on the vulnerability of flesh and the horrors of bodily violations. But even non-graphic horror films tend to trade in imaginative universes that prompt us to consider mortality. The horror of death is a crucial component in the great fear engine that powers the genre. Human consciousness is a double-edged sword—source of joy and wonder and of terror and pain. We realize that we are going to die eventually, and our art probes that brute fact like the tongue seeking a sore tooth.[35] We may not like to think about our own mortality, but we are incurably curious about death.

The extreme violence depicted or suggested in many horror movies unsettles us, both because the bodily mutilations are unpleasant to look at, and because many such films invite us to empathize with their victims and thus to mirror their pain. But we are also disturbed by the idea that the world contains supremely evil people (or nonhuman forces) who take great pleasure in inflicting pain on innocents. The horror scholar Xavier Aldana Reyes tells the story of the first time he saw the infamous horror film *Hostel*. That film, which was one of the first flicks to earn the label "torture porn," depicts a trio of tourists who are traveling in Europe and end up being captured by bad guys and sold to other bad guys for recreational torture and murder. We get some pretty gruesome scenes of explicit violence and physical torture. Aldana Reyes explains how those scenes made him squirm, but what really stayed with him was the film's premise: "I was horrified by the thought of [its] plausibility . . . and the possibility that people, somewhere in the world, would be mad enough to pay money to kill or torture someone they did not know for the mere pleasure of seeing someone suffer and die."[36]

Horrifying sights and disturbing ideas. Broken bodies, slobbering monsters, dark visions of mortality, and inhuman evil. It is the stuff of nightmares, and indeed, nightmares are a fairly commonly reported consequence of horror films. The scary stuff depicted in the film lodges and festers in your brain, sprouting new and terrifying growths as you are sleeping. But that is not necessarily a bad thing, because frightening dreams may serve an important function in terms of calibrating the fear system and making sure it works as it should.[37]

Nightmares and Horror Movies

There is a special relationship between nightmares and horror movies. Not only can horror movies cause nightmares; there are examples of nightmares having provided inspiration for horror movies. The 2014 movie *It Follows*, for instance, was inspired by director David Robert Mitchell's recurring childhood nightmare about "being followed by some sort of monster."[38] Mitchell took that nightmare and turned it into an evocative and genuinely terrifying slasher movie.

A curious case of the relationship between nightmares and horror movies is the 1984 slasher film *Nightmare on Elm Street*, featuring iconic Freddy Krueger, who stalks and kills his victims in their dreams. This movie seems to have been inspired by news items about the mysterious deaths of 18 Laotian refugees over a four-year period.[39] The refugees were all young and healthy and died suddenly in their sleep. A *New York Times* journalist covering the deaths cautiously suggested that nightmares may have killed the refugees. He wrote: "Although pathologists have been reluctant to advance it publicly, one possibility being explored is an obscure pattern described in medical literature as 'Oriental nightmare death syndrome,' in which death results from terror induced by a nightmare."[40] *Terror induced by a nightmare.* You can see why such a thing would pique a horror artist's imagination.

A nightmare is a threatening model of the world conjured up by the sleeping brain—essentially, a horror story in which the dreamer is usually the protagonist. Both horror and nightmares work by stimulating the fear system through threat simulations. A crucial difference is that people do not normally experience their nightmares as a simulation, but as reality. That is why it can be such a relief to wake up from a nightmare and realize that it was just a nasty simulation inflicted on you by your brain. You also cannot switch off or walk away from a nightmare. That element of control, along with the psychological distance provided by the knowledge that a horror film is not real, is lacking from the nightmare. That is why nightmares are no fun, in contrast to horror movies.

Research on nightmares suggests that they are extremely common—much more common than you might think. On average, people have hundreds, possibly thousands of nightmares per year, we just do not remember most of them.[41] Why are they so common? A neuroscientist, Antti Revonsuo, has an intriguing theory, which is supported by a lot of cross-cultural data on dream contents.[42] Revonsuo's idea is that the function of nightmares is threat simulation—rehearsal for disaster, sort of like a nightly fire drill. Revonsuo thinks that evolution has equipped the brain with a virtual reality engine that produces nightly simulations—including horrifying threat simulations that keep our threat detection and avoidance skills sharp. Much of the time that great engine is just quietly rumbling inside your head, producing neutral or positive dreams, but when it is stimulated—for instance when people face danger in their lives—the engine roars into life and blasts out horror stories. Those nightly horror stories serve an important function, Revonsuo says. They are not glitches in the system, they are a crucial survival mechanism.

Revonsuo's theory helps explain not just the prevalence of nightmares, but also the content of them. The most common dream threats cross-culturally come from animals and male strangers. Why is that? Most people do not spend day after day being chased by scary animals and creepy guys. However, across human prehistory, when the dream-production system evolved, animals and male strangers were main sources of mortality. The dream-production system is calibrated to a prehistoric world. It is sort of ironic, really. Humans have worked hard to construct an environment free of danger, developed technologies for building sturdy physical defenses, and harnessed the power of electricity in an effort to abolish the dark . . . yet still our ancient, ancestral foes hunt us in our nightmares, and in our horror stories.

Post-traumatic nightmares are common because traumatic incidents fuel the dream-production engine. If we find ourselves in a dangerous situation but manage to escape it, the system produces simulations of similar situations night after night, not unlike an army base stepping up security and increasing the frequency of emergency drills after an attack. This may be why horror movies sometimes cause nightmares. I am speculating here, but it may be that ancient defensive systems in your brain process the frightening stimuli in a horror movie as evidence of a live threat. The little scout in your brain registers threat and sends an urgent signal to the dream-production system. "DEFCON 4, guys, I'm getting reports of scary animals and/or creepy guys in the neighborhood. Let's stay frosty." The scout, who does not realize or does not care that the threat is fictional, senses that the world has suddenly turned dangerous, so he mobilizes defense systems that do what they can to keep you alive, which includes serving up nighttime threat scenarios. It may also be that bad dreams following horror movie exposure are merely a spillover effect from activation of the fear system. We don't know yet. Either way, knowing that nightmares are probably a crucial survival mechanism that may help you cope with real danger may ease the pain of a bad night's sleep, whether or not it is caused by a horror movie.

When Fear Is Fun

Clearly, fright reactions and lingering dread in response to horror movies are common. That should not really surprise anybody, and you can hardly blame horror movies for having those effects. That would be like blaming a comedy for making you laugh. Even so, media researchers who study horror have a tendency to forget that fear can be attractive and fun. One research article, which set out to investigate autobiographical memories of frightening films, started out by listing negative effects of exposure to violent and frightening films. The authors then said, "One of the clear negative effects of viewing violence and horror is fear."[43]

Well, duh. The whole point of a horror film is to feel fear. It is what people want, what they are implicitly or even explicitly promised by the film. Horror movie ad campaigns frequently emphasize a film's scariness as a mark of quality—the director's cut of *The Exorcist* was billed as "The Most Terrifying Movie Ever Made." And it is not just media researchers either. Psychologists who study fear also often forget that fear can be enjoyable. The psychologist Carroll Izard, who did pioneering work on human emotions, wrote that "fear is the most toxic of all the emotions."[44] It can be toxic, yes, but fear can also be the catalyst for pleasurable recreational activities.

In one study, my colleagues and I asked people—horror fans, horror haters, and everybody in between—about the kinds of emotions that they expect to feel from a horror movie.[45] Unsurprisingly, everybody expected to feel fear. The big difference between horror lovers and horror haters was in terms of expected *positive* emotions. Horror fans expect to feel joy, much more so than horror haters, and they expect to feel anticipation and surprise. They genuinely enjoy the playful engagement with negative emotions that horror movies offer. I have met many horror fans who enthusiastically trade anecdotes about films that "traumatized" them when they were kids. I put "traumatized" in quotation marks because we are not really talking about clinical trauma here. We are talking mild fright reactions, including the sleep disturbances and lingering dread that so concern the media psychologists. Well, horror fans are a bit like chili pepper enthusiasts. It has got to burn—that is a prerequisite for enjoyment. You do not want it to burn too much, obviously, and not too little, either—the trick is to hit the right dose of fear, to find the "sweet spot."[46]

Stephen Volk, the scriptwriter for *Ghostwatch*, was obviously distressed by those cases that I mentioned before. But he also got a lot of enthusiastic feedback from viewers who had been deeply frightened by the show. As Volk said in an interview: "The best result [was] people coming up and saying 'I had to sleep with the light on for three weeks but it got me into film-making' and some have said 'it got me into horror.'"[47] There is an element of artistic appreciation here. Even horror fans who are overwhelmed by fear, or who suffer unwanted effects, may feel genuine respect for the craftsmanship, the artistry, that went into the movie that scared them so.

Some of those media psychologists who study the negative effects of horror almost make it sound as if the horror industry is akin to the crystal meth industry—giving people what they crave and destroying them in the process. The thing is, the potential positive effects of horror have been almost completely ignored by media psychologists. If you go to a kindergarten and ask the kids to recall times when they got hurt during play, you are quickly going to get the impression that play is painful, dangerous business. Like play, though, horror can be fun and rewarding business. And it may even come with real benefits.

Positive Effects of Horror

There is not a lot of research on the positive social and psychological effects of horror movies. But one intriguing study, conducted in a haunted house attraction, found that a horror experience in a commercial haunted house had the effect of energizing people and of elevating their mood, especially among those individuals who had been in a fairly bad mood before the experience.[48]

The researchers behind this study do not know exactly what explains the mood improvement. It could be an unconscious contrast effect—after having witnessed horrifying events, your own life is likely to look pretty good in comparison. That looming exam paper is nothing compared to a raving chainsaw killer. Your going-on-busted carburetor really does not measure up to a fiery demon from hell. It could also be some kind of dopaminergic spillover—feel-good neurochemicals flooding the system. The physiological arousal produced by the haunted house experience may have extended beyond the haunt experience itself. Future research will have to determine the cause and see if the effect replicates and extends to other forms of horror than the haunted house in which the researchers collected their data. If the effect is solid, I would not be surprised to find that something similar happens for horror movie audiences.

I have often noticed how people leaving a movie theater after having watched a scary film are eagerly and happily interacting. They seem both energized and elated.

For most people, watching a horror movie is a social event.[49] It is something you do together, and a good chunk of the pleasure of watching a horror movie is social. It is responding in synchrony to the horrors on screen, it is responding to each other's responses, it is talking about the experience during and after. It is laughing together after you scream together. It is the sense of having gone through an intense experience together. I was on a research trip to Beijing in China some years back, and I got a chance to visit several haunted attractions. Like most American commercial haunted houses, people go through in groups of five or so. In one of the haunts, my Chinese guide and I were put in a group with two Chinese teenagers, both of whom were almost crying with fear as we went through— and jumping with delight afterward. When we emerged from the haunt, the three Chinese speakers were enthusiastically chatting like old buddies. Aptly, the haunt's slogan was: "You come as strangers and leave as friends."

Collective horror watching probably has bonding effects. Nobody has studied it systematically yet, but research from other fields suggests that the effect may exist. For example, research on so-called dysphoric high-arousal collective rituals—psychologically or physically painful rituals such as fire-walking—has found that such rituals make participants feel more connected. The experience boosts their sense of collective identity, of belonging together, and makes them more generous toward each other.[50] Likewise, a group of researchers found that when they exposed subjects to pain—making them hold their hands in icy water or squat for as long as possible, or eat hot chili peppers—those subjects felt more strongly connected to each other; they trusted each other more, and became more cooperative.[51]

Something similar could be taking place when groups of people watch horror movies together. It is a shared, high-intensity dysphoric experience designed for emotional synchronization. More than that, though, it is a shared *aesthetic* experience, and people enjoy collectively responding to, and discussing their responses to, aesthetic stimuli. They go to concerts and museums together. And they certainly watch horror movies together—not just because watching a horror movie with others is less scary (which is not necessarily the case, as we will see), but because shared experience is inherently pleasurable. Hopefully, future research will tell us more about the social effects of collective horror movie watching—and I will return to the issue in the last chapter.

There is one particular kind of bonding that has been studied a bit in the domain of horror movie watching: romantic bonding. Indeed, some scientific evidence suggests that watching a horror movie on a date is not a bad idea. Moviemakers have known this for a while; many slasher films back in the 1980s were actually marketed as date movies.[52] As a movie industry insider said in 1980, at the height of the slasher film craze: "You can never go wrong with a movie that makes a girl move closer to her date."[53] Strikingly, a study on autobiographical memories found that out of 233 participants, 230 could recollect having been to a horror movie on a date.[54]

Consequently, media researchers have proposed a so-called snuggle theory of horror. If you are watching a horror movie with a date, it is not unlikely that the scary events on screen will make you move closer together, perhaps compel one sweaty hand to find another in the darkness of the movie theater, and mutual attraction may even be boosted. The body goes into a state of heightened arousal that may be misinterpreted as, well, erotic attraction.[55] "My heart is hammering away and my palms are sweaty. Is it the movie? Or the person sitting next to me?"

But there is more to snuggle theory. It is also the idea that horror movies provide a context for young people to demonstrate socially sanctioned, gender-appropriate responses in the face of emotionally demanding material.[56] Males are expected to display mastery; females distress. One study, published in 1986, showed a clip from *Friday the 13th, Part III* to pairs of undergraduate students. In each pair, one was an unsuspecting research subject while the other was a confederate—that is, somebody who was secretly in cahoots with the researchers. The confederates varied their behavior in different trials, exhibiting either mastery or distress (or nothing at all).

Interestingly, male subjects said they enjoyed the gory clip more when their female co-viewer responded with distress, whereas female subjects enjoyed the clip more when their male co-viewer responded with mastery. There was even a tendency for female subjects to find their male co-viewers more attractive when they responded with mastery rather than distress, and vice versa. That curious effect was not found for exceptionally attractive co-viewers, though, only for "persons less blessed with great physique."[57] Apparently, some men enjoy an opportunity for displaying bravery and an ability to protect a distressed woman, whereas some women—who, as we have seen, tend to react more fearfully to horror movies—enjoy having a cool and collected male co-viewer to help them make it through the ordeal. That enjoyment may then color their evaluation of the attractiveness of their co-viewer.

It is a fun study, but it is also old, and much has happened since 1986. Gender roles have softened somewhat, and gender-typical behavioral displays may have become less attractive. Also, the researchers had a fairly small pool of subjects (36 males and 36 females), and they showed only a short clip on a 19-inch television screen in a lab setting. That is quite different from watching an entire horror movie in a theater or at home. A bigger study, involving more subjects, could paint a different picture. Even so, you could do worse than take your date to a horror movie. And of all the questions you can ask on a first date, "Do you like horror movies?" is just about the most predictive of a good match: if you and your date respond the same, that is a pretty good indicator of relationship compatibility.[58] (That discovery was made by Sam Yagan, a cofounder of the dating site OkCupid, when he trawled through his users' responses to a range of match questions and correlated them with relationship success.)

Conceivably, horror movies help us practice coping strategies. Nobody has systematically investigated such an effect, though. We know from other research that people use a range of coping strategies for fear regulation, and as I mentioned in the introduction, my colleagues and I studied fear regulation strategies among visitors in a haunted attraction.[59] We went to a haunted house with a small army of research assistants and recruited participants from among the visitors. Our participants were given a challenge to either maximize or minimize their own fear as they walked through the haunt. We then interviewed the guests to learn about the strategies they had used for up- or down-regulating fear.

As it turns out, our participants actively used a wide range of strategies—cognitive, behavioral, and social ones. The people trying to keep fear down would remind themselves that it was just a set with actors in makeup. They would try to distract themselves, they would cover their ears or eyes, and they would stay close to group members. The people looking to maximize fear did the opposite— except for that social strategy, which was identical in both groups. People trying to keep fear down stay close to others and seek contact, but people trying to become as afraid as possible *also* seek contact with other, equally frightened people. The strategy works in both directions because people feel safer when they are together, but fear is contagious. Presumably, whether the strategy works to suppress or enhance fear depends on such factors as context and mindset.

The point is this: horror consumers are not just passive spectators. Instead, they seem to actively use strategies for achieving the right level of fear. So could it be that frequent horror users become more adept at regulating their own fear? It is an empirical question—it is something we can investigate scientifically—but it has not attracted much research yet. But my colleagues and I did a study on pandemic preparedness and horror film watching in which we found that horror fans experienced less psychological distress than non-fans during the COVID-19 pandemic (I'll return to that study in a later chapter).[60] So it may be that horror buffs are better at regulating their own fear than non-buffs, but we do not know much about the extent to which that ability carries over into non-recreational contexts, that is, whether horror buffs are also better at keeping nervousness down when they are waiting for a job interview or walking home alone at night.

The idea that horror movies help us cope with real fears probably is not as far-fetched as it may sound. In a later chapter, we will talk about how horror films can help us confront large-scale sociocultural fears, but it may also be the case that we get better at managing personal fear through horror. I have even heard the startling claim that people who suffer from clinical anxiety can get relief from watching horror movies. In recent years, such claims have made the news, with headlines such as "Why Some Anxious People Find Comfort in Horror Movies,"[61] "Why Some People with Anxiety Love Watching Horror Movies,"[62] and "The Power of Horror Films as a Cure for Anxiety."[63] The thing is, these articles, and the many others like them, are not based on scientific findings. They are largely anecdotal, but often supported by expert testimony from fear researchers. The basic idea is that somebody with anxiety can alleviate that anxiety, or make it manageable, by confronting negative emotions in controlled and controllable doses through scary media. Your day-to-day life is simmering with low-key dread, but the blast of horror that you get from a movie is something you have chosen and something you can reject. It is also a way of feeling fear and anxiety with a well-defined source and a rationale—it is okay to feel fear when you are watching horror; it is sanctioned fear and mandated anxiety.

Until the alleged therapeutic uses of horror films for individuals with anxiety disorders have been clinically examined and documented, I would not recommend scary movies as a remedy for anybody suffering from anxiety. It could very well be that they work—indeed, the anecdotal evidence is compelling, and we are currently running several research projects to investigate this issue—but it is also plausible that self-medicating with horror movies could backfire. In connection with a research project, I interviewed haunted house guests who had to prematurely discontinue their haunt experience because they were overwhelmed by fear. (Most haunts have a safe word or gesture that tells the actors and sometimes hidden guards that you want out.) As it turned out, several of those tap-outs suffered from anxiety disorder. Many of them were in tears, and some of them unable to talk to me. Anxiety disorders are serious business. Anybody with an anxiety disorder who wants to take a stab at watching a horror movie should begin with some very mild fare indeed.

So, even though short- and long-term negative (but mild) effects of horror movies have been well established by researchers, we know little about positive effects. I think it is highly likely that such effects exist—for example, bonding effects and maybe improved coping skills—and I think that the negative effects have been exaggerated in the research literature. It is not that they do not exist, it is that they are not necessarily as obviously bad as the researchers seem to suggest. Humans do weird and apparently painful things, such as shower in water that is slightly too hot and watch horror movies. Yes, it hurts, but that is the whole point.

What Can You Do?

If you are still nervous about being messed up by horror movies, let me assure you that the odds of losing one's mind solely because of a horror movie are practically zero. A healthy mind is more resilient than one might imagine, and I have found no clinically documented cases of "cinematic neurosis" in individuals without serious psychological or psychiatric issues. Of course, you cannot expect to watch a horror movie without some psychological pain. Unpleasant psychological states—fear, anxiety, dread—are part of the deal and, indeed, at the very source of recreational fear, just as the chemical compound capsaicin, a natural irritant, is at the source of the buzz of eating hot peppers. In the domain of horror, fear is a prerequisite for fun.

The trick is to find something that hits your sweet spot in terms of fear level, as we have seen. It should not be too tame, but not too intense, either. People have different sweet spots, so some introspection and trial are called for. For example, I know that Japanese and South Korean supernatural horror movies get me bad. I know this because I watched a couple such films—*Ringu* from 1998 and *Dark Water* from 2002—and found them to be overwhelmingly frightening. (Actually, I never finished *Dark Water*. I am probably going to pick it up again one of these days. Maybe.) So I am always a little wary of new horror movie releases from the Far East. So if something in your constitution makes you particularly susceptible to a certain kind of horror, maybe stay away from it or at least approach it carefully. Do not watch *Arachnophobia* if you are afraid of spiders. If your biggest fear is ghosts, maybe start out with a psychological horror film about a serial killer. If injury and injection stuff makes you lightheaded, avoid splatter movies. Try to figure out where your limit is, and how scary a given film is, for example by reading reviews before watching it.

If it is mainly sleep disturbances such as nightmares that you are worried about, perhaps it helps to realize that nightmares do not seem to be bugs in the system—bad code in the neural networks—but are likely to be adaptive threat simulations. Those nighttime horror shows evolved for a reason. Still, you may find it useful—as I do—to employ a mental palate cleanser. If you have watched a horror movie at night and are about ready to go to bed, set aside 10 minutes to watch a so-called fail video on YouTube, a video about penguins slipping on ice, say, or cats being jerks. Something funny and light. It scrubs the worst of the immediate horror from your mind.

If you do watch something that overwhelms you with fear—gives you nightmares, makes you hypervigilant—watch it again. And again. Learn everything you can about the film. It may sound counterintuitive, but the trick is to create some distance between yourself and the film, and to approach it as an aesthetic artifact—as fiction, a construction, rather than reality. The more you watch the film, the more boring it becomes, and the easier it is for you to start paying attention to how it is made—how it uses music to create dread, for example, or how cinematography and editing create suspense. Most movies in the so-called Hollywood style (and that is most movies, no matter where they are produced) are designed to create an illusion of continuity for maximum immersion. You are supposed to be sucked into the movie and forget it is a construction; you are not, generally speaking, supposed to notice style, such as patterns of editing or the interplay between diegetic and nondiegetic sound. But if you watch a movie many times, it becomes less engaging, in terms of immersion, and you can begin to pay attention to form. Try to analyze the movie, especially the most frightening scenes. How are they shot? How are lighting and sound used to create a particular effect? What about special effects? Once you get an analytical fix on the movie, its power to frighten you diminishes. Conversely, before you watch a horror movie, learn as much as possible about it. Read up on how the movie was conceived, study details of the shooting, read interviews with the cast and crew. It helps you approach the movie as an aesthetic artifact. And as you are watching, rest assured that your sanity is not endangered.

4

"I'm Nervous about Horror Films and My Physical Health"

If you are worried about the effect of horror movies on your physical health, I have mainly good news for you. It is true that people have suffered physically as a result of exposure to horror, and a few people seem to have died of fright as they were watching horror movies, but such occurrences are extremely rare and not something most of us should worry about. There may even be health benefits from horror exposure.

How can you be hurt by a horror movie? Well, recall that cinema patrons fainted in droves in response to *The Exorcist*, and a few of those unfortunates hurt themselves pretty badly. In fact, one guy threw a $350,000 lawsuit at the distributor, Warner Bros. He fainted during the movie and broke his jaw when he collided with the seat in front of him, claiming that a subliminal image of a "death mask" was to blame.[1]

It is true that a creepy face is flashed very briefly at several points in the film (Fig. 4.1), but it is not subliminal, just very fleeting. (For a stimulus to be subliminal, it has to fall under the threshold of conscious perception—that is, you do not consciously register it.) And William Peter Blatty, author of the novel and producer of the film, had been head of the policy branch of the US Air Force's Psychological Warfare Division. Blatty had almost certainly come across the alleged power of subliminal messages, and may have put that knowledge into practice in the film. Anyway, whether the semi-subliminal death mask caused the plaintiff to faint, I don't know. And the lawsuit, to my knowledge, was settled out of court.

Figure 4.1 *The Exorcist* (Warner Bros., directed by William Friedkin, 1973) infamously used semi-subliminal images to terrify audience members. This creepy image—actress Eileen Dietz in demonic makeup—is flashed very briefly at key points in the movie. One moviegoer sued Warner Bros. because he'd gotten hurt when he fainted during the film and blamed the semi-subliminal images.

Also from the Department of People Getting Hurt by Horror, there is an ailment known in the medical literature as "Stephen King wrist." It was described in the *Western Medical Journal* in 1999.[2] A 51-year-old woman complained to her doctor of wrist pains. It turned out that the woman had been reading the "latest Stephen King thriller" in bed (probably King's lengthy 1998 ghost/romance story *Bag of Bones*) and had been using her left hand to prop up the novel for several hours each night. The result was painful wrist strain. Her doctor ordered her to "stop this reading practice for a few nights" and then "alternate hands in holding such tomes" or get a portable podium on which to place the book. The patient took the doctor's advice and the pain disappeared.

Certainly, watching a horror movie can be painful—psychologically, as we have seen, but also physically. As we learned in a previous chapter, the jolt of a jump scare can be physically unpleasant, like a mild electric shock. And the extreme tension produced by accomplished scenes of suspense can be exhausting. There can also be intense physical discomfort associated with scenes of body violations—watching an eyeball being sliced open, for example, or a fingernail being torn off.[3] That stuff is unpleasant to even think about. When we see somebody else getting hurt, the mechanism of somatic empathy—a mirroring of another's physical sensations—makes us register their pain on our own bodies, albeit in a watered-down version. Seeing a fingernail being torn off is unpleasant, but certainly less unpleasant than having a fingernail torn off. The phenomenon has been called "sensation mimicry"[4] (it is related to the affective mimicry that I mentioned earlier), and gory horror movies depend on this phenomenon for their effect on the audience.

If a horror movie *really* gets under your skin, you may experience symptoms of panic—a powerful sensation of imminent doom, a fear of losing control, passing out, running out of air. Panic shades into dread when it is the panic itself you fear—that is, you come to dread your own reaction. I remember feeling a stirring of real dread when I saw *The Blair Witch Project* back when it came out. I saw the movie in a theater. Toward the end of the picture, when the remaining two protagonists go into a creepy, abandoned (but maybe not empty) house in the woods, my heart was racing and I felt like I was becoming untethered from reality. The tension was reaching a crescendo and the atmosphere of utter dread was climaxing. The guy next to me had been muttering frantically for a while, and his muttering became increasingly agitated and unintelligible. I thought I was probably going to pass out if this crap didn't end soon. (I did not, and it did, but there was a moment of near-panic there.) No panic attack for me, but I think I came fairly close, and I cannot help but admire the film for it. *The Blair Witch Project* remains one of my favorite horror movies.

So, unpleasant physical sensations are par for the course, and in a few, isolated cases, people have gotten hurt as a result of horror movie watching. What is the worst that can happen, though? Death-by-horror?

Can a Horror Movie Kill You?

The eminent physiologist Walter B. Cannon, who in 1915 coined the phrase "fight-or-flight response,"[5] was intensely interested in the physiological pathways of fear. He took an interest in so-called voodoo deaths late in his career and published a paper on the phenomenon in 1942.[6] In this paper, he described anecdotal cases of voodoo deaths—"primitive" people from tribes around the world being smitten by black magic and then dying within a few days.

Cannon argued that there is a perfectly natural explanation for these apparently supernatural deaths. Since the victims believed in black magic, being "cursed" by a powerful voodoo priest frightened them mightily. The massive release of adrenaline may have resulted in damage to the circulatory system and internal organs, and the sheer dread of knowing that death is fast approaching may have caused victims to cease their food and drink intake, which contributed to their physical deterioration and eventual demise. Subsequent studies suggest that Cannon got it basically right (even though the hormones involved in the fight-or-flight response had not been discovered when he was working).[7] So, yes, you can die from fright.

The annals of medicine have several cases of what appears to be death from fright. For example, in 1846, the esteemed medical journal *The Lancet* carried a tragic case report titled "Notes of a Case of Death from Fright." The item described a medical case "in which death seemed attributable solely to fright." A healthy two-year-old, Elizabeth S, was taken on the arm of an older girl into a candy store. While they were inside, a little boy wearing a "red 'Guy-Fawkes' mask" appeared outside the window, giving little Elizabeth a terrible shock. She said she thought it was "the Bogie." She started trembling violently, her face "expressive of great terror, and her hair wet with perspiration." Her health deteriorated over the following days, and after 12 days, she woke up in the middle of the night, crying "Bogie, bogie!" When she suffered seizures, a doctor was summoned. He tried to treat her. The treatments did not work, and the next day the girl died.[8] She was autopsied, and the cause of death ruled to be "fright."

So, while it is possible to die from fright, I have not found scientifically documented cases of horror movie viewers dying because of the film. There are anecdotal news items, such as the story of a middle-aged man suffering a heart attack in the middle of *Jaws*, but it is hard to tell what, exactly, caused it.

Similarly, the newspaper *Times of India* has carried a couple of articles about apparent cases of death from horror movie fright. In 2010, a bunch of boarding school students got together for a horror film marathon. During one of the movies, a student "went to the bathroom and came out screaming in shock." He collapsed and was taken to the hospital, where he was declared dead.[9] And in 2016, two men went to catch *The Conjuring 2* in the local movie theater. One of the men, a 65-year-old, started to complain of chest pains and then passed out during the climax of the film. He was declared dead at the hospital. And, in a bizarre turn of events, the hospital staff asked his friend to bring the corpse to another hospital for a postmortem—but the friend disappeared with the corpse somewhere along the way.[10]

We cannot draw any strong conclusions from such news items, which are skimpy on the details. In theory it is possible to be killed by the fright provoked by a horror movie, I suppose, but it is extremely unlikely for a healthy person to meet the Grim Reaper in this way. In my opinion, it is not worth worrying about. Let us focus instead on potential positive health effects of horror movies.

Can Horror Movies Be Good for Your Physical Health?

The potential health benefits of horror movies have not been rigorously tested, but every now and then a news story about such benefits makes the rounds online. For example, in 2012—just before Halloween—a news item popped up claiming that watching horror movies is a good way to burn calories.[11] The story reported on a study conducted by a scientist who had asked test subjects to watch horror movies while he measured energy expenditure. The finding: horror movies burn calories quite effectively—and the most effective of the 10 films tested was Kubrick's *The Shining*, which torched 184 calories. Next on the list was *Jaws*, with 161 calories burned, followed by *The Exorcist* with 158 calories.

That is a cool finding, but this study was not published in the usual scientific channels, which means it has not undergone peer review (the standard process of ensuring the scientific quality of academic publications by having other experts evaluate them before publication). And the sample was very small—only 10 individuals. In fact, the study was commissioned by a now-defunct British video rental service, presumably as a Halloween gimmick. That does not mean that its findings are not true, but it does mean that we should not draw strong conclusions from the study. Besides, the finding is not really that surprising. Of course you burn calories when you are watching a horror movie—just as you do when you are sleeping, or on the toilet, or whatever—and it seems plausible that the mild stress induced by a horror movie has metabolic effects. But you will not hear your physician prescribe horror movies in place of physical exercise anytime soon, I don't think.

To complicate the situation even more, any metabolic benefits of watching horror may be offset by overeating prompted by the movie. A study from 1992 found that "restrained eaters"—people who carefully limit their food intake to avoid becoming obese—were more likely to overeat if they watched a horror movie than if they watched a neutral movie or a funny movie.[12]

In this study, 91 female college students were recruited to watch a 20-minute clip from a movie. Their food intake restraint scores were measured, they were each given a bag containing 400 grams of salted and buttered popcorn, and they were then shown a movie clip—either from an emotionally neutral film (a travelogue), a positive film (a funny clip of the candid camera variety), or a negative film (a clip from John Carpenter's classic slasher movie *Halloween*). After the clip, each bag was weighed and food intake calculated. The scientists found that for the women who watched the horror clip, the more restrained they were, the more popcorn they ate—on average about 50 grams of popcorn for the high-restraint eaters versus about 20 grams on average for the low-restraint eaters. Moreover, highly restrained eaters who watched the horror clip gobbled much more popcorn than highly restrained eaters who watched the neutral clip and the funny clip. Somehow, the horror movie made them relax their restraint.

Conversely, though, unrestrained eaters watching the horror clip ate less popcorn than unrestrained eaters watching the comedy or the neutral clip. So, if you are very careful about your food intake— a restrained eater—and you are looking to watch a horror movie, perhaps limit the snacks you bring to the party. If you are an unrestrained eater looking to lose a few pounds, though, you are better off watching a horror flick than a travel movie or a comedy.

Another study—this one from 2003—set out to investigate whether witnessing a "fictitious stressful event" had any effect on leukocyte production, that is, whether watching a horror movie causes the body to produce more white blood cells.[13] The body produces white blood cells under stress. That is part of the body's first line of defense—the immune system—and serves to fight disease and infection. So the researchers' thesis was that the stress induced by a fictitious event might show a similar result.

The researchers split their subjects into two groups. One group watched a horror movie—Tobe Hooper's infamous *The Texas Chain Saw Massacre* from 1974—and the other group sat in a boring room, doing nothing. Blood samples were taken before, during, and after the session. Lo and behold, the participants who watched the horror film actually had an increase in white blood cell count. Apparently, horror movies do cause a short-term boost to the immune system. That sounds like a good thing, but as scientists like to say, more research is needed. Maybe this artificial stimulation of the immune system results in a temporary weakening of the system afterward. We do not know yet.

A fun little study from 2015, published in the medical journal *The BMJ*, proposed to investigate whether fear does, indeed, curdle the blood, as the saying has it.[14] The scientists behind the study recruited a small sample of participants and asked half of them to watch first a horror film (James Wan's *Insidious* from 2010) and then, a week later, a boring documentary movie. The other half watched the same films, but in reverse order. Blood samples were taken before, in between movies, and after.

The researchers then looked at changes in blood coagulant—a protein that clots or "curdles" the blood—and found that yes, the acute fear caused by the horror movie did indeed release blood coagulants. Why? Because when the organism is under threat, it releases not only leukocytes, as we have seen, but also coagulants. It is a defense mechanism, a way of readying the organism for injury by attempting to reduce blood loss. Is that good or bad? Well, it is difficult to say. I guess it is good if you accidentally cut yourself when you are watching a horror movie, but the researchers behind the study also note that too much coagulant in the blood may be associated with increased risk of venous thrombosis (a blood clot in a vein). However, the study only involved 21 participants, which makes it a little tricky to draw substantive conclusions.

What about physical well-being? Nobody has investigated that empirically in the context of horror movies, but maybe we can get a few hints from research on painful rituals. A fascinating 2019 study looked at the effects of extreme ritual practices on well-being, and found that people who engage in such rituals—typically painful religious rituals—reported that their health improved as a result.[15] We are talking extreme suffering here: walking on fire, piercing one's skin with big instruments, that sort of thing. I mentioned in the previous chapter that such rituals may have bonding effects, but they seem also to have a positive effect on self-perceived physical health. The feel-better effect reported by the participants in the study is probably due partly to a release of neurotransmitters—such as the body's own painkiller, endorphin—during the ordeal. Partly, it is probably a result of psychological recalibration: having endured the stress and pain of the ritual steels people for enduring similar ordeals in life. As the scientists put it, "Age-old cultural practices that seem risky, unpleasant, or dangerous can have real-life consequences for their practitioners by utilizing pain and suffering as strategies of resilience and coping with environmental stressors."[16]

These researchers say nothing about horror movies, and to be sure, even the most freaky horror film is less painful than the religious rituals they describe. But maybe their findings generalize to the cultural practice of threat simulation. Maybe horror movies improve physical well-being, just as they may boost one's mood. Again: more research is needed.

So, to sum up, you should not be too worried about your physical health in connection with horror movies. In fact, there is at least suggestive evidence that horror movies may have some positive health effects. Being in a state of stress for a long period of time is harmful to the organism, but little bursts of controllable stress—like those supplied by a horror movie—seem to be harmless and may even be beneficial.

5

"I'm Nervous That Horror Films Are Immoral"

We have talked about the effects of horror movies on mental and physical health. What, then, about *spiritual* health? Do horror movies corrupt the soul, in a manner of speaking? What is the effect on the viewer's moral compass of watching movies such as *Chopping Mall* or *I Spit on Your Grave*? Are such movies immoral? Do they turn people into callous connoisseurs of depravity and evil?

The short answer is no. There is no evidence, not even indirect evidence, that horror movies create psychopaths. It is too early to skip ahead to the next chapter, though. The issue of horror movies and morality is complex—partly because the genre *itself* is complex and often has a complex engagement with moral issues, partly because the relationship between horror movies and moral psychology is complex. We do not watch an immoral horror movie and become immoral, and we do not watch a horror movie with a liberal subtext and become liberal. Much of the concern over the moral effects of horror—and violent entertainment more generally—arises from a naive understanding of human nature and the psychology of media use; a "monkey watch, monkey do" sort of understanding. We do not passively absorb media entertainment; we engage actively and often critically with it.

Horror movies are good at raising moral hackles because such movies often depict fraught subjects like violence and sex, and because they have a reputation for being sensationalistic, if not outright exploitative. Horror is by definition about bad stuff—death, pain, monstrosity, evil, fear, terror—and some people are concerned about what it does to viewers to look at depictions of bad stuff.

Indeed, modern cultural history has seen several moral panics focused on the horror genre.

Most recently, cultural critics have taken aim at movies in the torture porn subgenre—a type of horror movie that dwells on explicit and realistic depictions of bodily mutilation and intense suffering. But long before the widely publicized controversies over torture porn, in the 1980s, there were public debates about "video nasties"— which led to actual legislation—and about allegedly misogynistic "women-in-danger films." And before that, in the 1950s, widespread concerns over the moral ramifications of horror comic book reading led to Senate hearings and self-imposed censorship in the comics industry.[1] And before that, in the nineteenth century, many Victorians were deeply concerned about the effects of the exceptionally popular penny dreadfuls, which were cheap, serialized stories—costing a penny per installment—which focused on crime and other frightening subjects. And before that . . . well, people have *always* been concerned about the moral effects of frightening and violent entertainment,[2] and about the moral habitus of people who choose to seek out such entertainment when there is plenty of entertainment in the world without frightening or violent content.

Torture Porn, Video Nasties, and Slasher Films

The term "torture porn" was coined by the film critic David Edelstein, who in a 2006 essay for *New York Magazine* wondered at the sudden profusion of ultraviolent, graphic, gory movies at the multiplex.[3] Edelstein focused on *Hostel*, Eli Roth's low-budget 2006 movie about a group of backpackers who are captured by evil Eastern Europeans and sold to rich people for torture and death. Roth depicts this torture in nauseating detail—the slicing of a character's Achilles' tendon, the application of a blowtorch to another character's eye, and so on. The movie became a massive hit, grossing some $82 million worldwide, despite its tiny $4.8 million budget and despite—or, more likely, at least in part because—its explicitness. It is a well-made film, with respectable production values, pretty interesting characters, and an engrossing plot with moments of real suspense. The torture scenes are incredibly painful to watch.

Edelstein recognized that there is nothing new about movies focusing in excruciating detail on explicit and realistic violence. What was new, according to him, was that these films—which had their heyday from around 2003, with the release of *Saw*, to 2008—were mainstream Hollywood productions achieving mainstream theatrical release. Edelstein was not so much interested in morally condemning *Hostel* and its ilk; he was genuinely perplexed by these films' popularity. As he wrote: "I'm baffled by how far this new stuff goes—and by why America seems so nuts these days about torture." Edelstein answered his own question by pointing to topical discussions about the morality of torture in the wake of 9/11 and the war on terror, with its so-called enhanced interrogation techniques. Many others have made that same connection. Torture was on people's minds, as was an awareness of personal physical vulnerability in an age of terror.[4]

Others were more willing to condemn this subgenre of horror movie—to accuse it of being shallow, in bad taste, even dangerous. Kira Cochrane, a British journalist writing for *The Guardian*, in 2007 denounced the "new subgenre of horror films which are so dehumanising, nasty and misogynist that they are collectively known either as 'gorno' (a conflation of 'gory' and 'porno'), or, more commonly, as 'torture porn.'"[5] Lenore Skenazy, an American writer and blogger, similarly expressed deep concern over torture porn that same year. As she wrote: "If we start accepting this kind of movie as just 'extreme' horror, the baseline will change. What once seemed out of line will become mainstream." She proceeded to make a call for action:

> Let's insist on a new rating, such as NC-25 when films involve sexual torture, so teens can't hand the producers their allowance. Or let's promise to boycott not only the torture movie itself but also any future movies the stars make, so they have zero incentive to appear in a film like this. Or let's just find the producers and hang them upside down and take out a dental drill and . . .
>
> Oh wait! That's not acceptable behavior. Yet.[6]

That last bit is telling. Skenazy is suggesting that unless we do something to eradicate torture porn movies, their audiences will become homicidal maniacs—that there is a direct causal link between watching torture porn and becoming deranged. And that is a dubious proposition, both because there is no evidence to support such a strong causality and because torture porn movies are more morally complicated than Skenazy (and Cochrane) makes them out to be. It is not just journalists and pundits, either. Torture porn and slasher movies have been condemned from a philosophical point of view for being immoral, on the assumption that such movies invite identification with the bad guys and erode audiences' capacities for compassion and empathy.[7] That, too, is a dubious proposition.[8]

The horror scholar Steve Jones has carefully examined the aesthetics and moral structure of torture porn and arrived at the conclusion that such movies typically encourage audiences to sympathize with the victims of torture, not the perpetrators (Fig. 5.1).[9] Such movies may even prompt audiences to reflect on moral quandaries, for instance by depicting sympathetic protagonists resorting to

Figure 5.1 So-called torture porn movies generated a lot of controversy because of their unflinching depiction of gory gruesomeness, but many such movies invite the audience to empathize with the victims of this gruesomeness, not the perpetrators. In Eli Roth's *Hostel* (Lionsgate, 2005), for instance, the central torture scene is highly focused on the anguished facial expression of protagonist Paxton (Jay Hernandez), encouraging the audience to share his pain (rather than the perverse pleasure of his torturer).

violence to escape their torturers, or to exact vengeance on them. There is a savage pleasure in watching victimized protagonists getting a violent comeuppance that may be ethically problematic, and which we will revisit when we talk about rape-revenge films. However, many of the most hostile detractors of torture porn forgot that it matters *how* violence is represented. There are many ways in which you can depict violence—there is a big difference between watching Tom getting his ass kicked by Jerry and watching somebody being beaten up in a Tarantino or a Peckinpah movie. Torture porn movies tend to depict violence as deeply unattractive and revolting, if sometimes morally justified as a last-resort measure, for instance when protagonists use violence to escape their tormentors.

A good deal of the mass-media concern over torture porn grew out of an assumption that gratuitous violence on film was becoming increasingly widespread and thus acceptable—that before long, mainstream Hollywood movies would become gory exercises in nihilistic mayhem. It does not look like the short-lived popularity of torture porn did much to increase the amount of on-screen gore in horror movies, though.

A pair of researchers, Blair Davis and Kial Natale, set out to investigate whether horror movies have become more or less gory recently. They selected 100 theatrically distributed American horror films from a 10-year period ranging from 1998 to 2007 (thus including most of the heyday of torture porn) and coded on-screen gore.[10] In other words, they watched those movies with a spreadsheet open in front of them, making a note every time something gory occurred on screen. They found that on-screen acts of gory violence had indeed increased slightly in that 10-year period, but only by an average of 40 seconds or so per film. A few incredibly gore-happy films, like Rob Zombie's controversial 2003 movie *House of 1000 Corpses* with its more than 18 minutes of on-screen gore, dragged up the average.

Across the whole period, the average per-film duration of on-screen gore was 235.79 seconds. That is about four minutes. Out of those four minutes, the bulk of gore was "passive gore"—that is, depictions of the aftermath of violence. Blood splatter on a wall, say, or a severed limb. The films had an average of 50 seconds of "active gore," that is, depictions of bodily violations. That is really not a lot for a feature-length movie.

So, given the way in which violence in torture porn is typically depicted as revolting, the moral outrage inspired by the subgenre seems to have been overblown. Horror scholars like Jones came to the genre's defense, showing it to be less shallow and more morally complex than many detractors assumed. Some scholars even suggested that torture porn may be therapeutic. Eli Roth himself said that he had heard from American soldiers stationed in Iraq that *Hostel* was wildly popular at American bases, letting soldiers blow off steam and show fear and horror in a socially sanctioned context (unlike the battlefield, where you have to stay frosty at all times).[11] The film scholar Isabel Pinedo likewise claimed that torture porn "helps us process violent and traumatic collective experience."[12] Pinedo does not offer any empirical evidence to support the claim, and there are no scientific studies that I know of that investigate it, unfortunately. But such an effect might well exist. Fiction does allow us to confront difficult emotions and situations in a sandboxed way, so to speak—through simulation.

In retrospect, it may look like the early 2000s were the Age of Torture Porn in American horror movie history. That is not really the case, though. Those movies got a lot of press, but they did not figure that prominently at the box office. The sociologist Todd Platts and I analyzed the 117 horror movies that reached the top 100 in domestic grosses in the North American film market in the period 2006–2016.[13] We then divided those movies into subgenres by consulting various trade publications and newspapers. We found that only about 5% of the horror movies reaching the top 100 were torture porn flicks. (By far the most popular subgenre was supernatural horror, which accounted for almost 40%.) In other words, torture porn does not really seem to be the face of the modern American horror film.

Torture porn has its cinematic roots in splatter movies—gory, grisly, low-budget horror films shown in grindhouse theaters or distributed on VHS tapes. Splatter movies, especially the kind that the excitable yellow press in Britain called "video nasties," really upset a lot of people back in the 1980s. Almost simultaneously, some in-fluential American film critics expressed worries over the rise of "women-in-danger" films, which depicted young women being stalked by bad guys and allegedly invited the audience to identify with the bad guys.

In the UK, newspaper stories about the availability and immo-rality of exploitation horror movies started appearing in 1982.[14] The *Sunday Times* ran a story in May 1982 headlined "How High Street Horror Is Invading the Home"—the story that coined the phrase "video nasty." Public concern over the ease with which children and youngsters could get their hands on VHS movies with upsetting ma-terial grew rapidly. The tabloid newspaper *Daily Mail* started a reg-ular crusade under the heading "Ban the Sadist Videos," calling for regulation of video content. One such story was headlined "Rape of Our Children's Minds."[15]

The video nasties were mainly American and Italian low-budget movies—for example, the Italian Nazi exploitation film *SS Experiment Camp* from 1976. This notorious film gleefully depicted sexual experiments on female prisoners in concentration camps. The film was eventually deemed illegal, in violation of the British Obscene Publications Act. The Obscene Publications Squad—a branch of the Scotland Yard—conducted raids on video stores to identify, impound, and destroy video nasties, which were "burned by the lorryload."[16] And in 1984, the campaign resulted in the Video Recordings Act, which made it illegal to sell or supply films that had not been examined and classified by the British Board of Film Classification. The video nasty controversies flared up again in 1993, when the yellow press suggested that the horrifying murder of two-year-old James Bulger by two 10-year-olds in Merseyside, UK, was inspired by *Child's Play 3* (featuring the murderous doll Chucky). The police found no evidence of such a link—and no evidence that the perpetrators had even seen the film.[17]

In the United States, the popular film review show *Sneak Previews*—hosted by movie critics Gene Siskel and Roger Ebert—featured a special segment about what Siskel and Ebert called women-in-danger films.[18] This segment, which aired in 1980, expressed deep concern about the apparent popularity of slasher and rape-revenge movies that seemed to encourage the audience to identify with a misogynistic killer. Such movies, according to Siskel and Ebert, played to mainly male audiences' sadistic desire to see nubile women punished by shady assailants. (Subsequent research has found that young women made up a significant portion of the audience for early slasher movies. Almost half of the tickets to *Halloween* and *Friday the 13th* had been sold to people under the age of 17, 55% of whom were female.)[19] They gave anecdotes of male cinemagoers apparently identifying with the killer and "cheering him on." Siskel and Ebert denounced these movies, suggesting that they were a pernicious backlash to the growth of feminism in the United States. In contrast to the video nasties campaign in the UK, however, Siskel and Ebert's campaign did not lead to legislation. But it did put a bright spotlight on a "disturbing trend at the movie box office," as they said.

Were the people concerned about video nasties and allegedly misogynistic slasher movies completely off the rails? Well, although many such films undoubtedly went "right off the map of good taste," as Roger Ebert said, claims about the detrimental effects of such movies were exaggerated or even unfounded, just as with the torture porn controversies. But I can only applaud an attempt to call out overt misogyny in movies, and it does make sense to try to shield kids from Nazi exploitation films. Personally, I would not show such a film to a 12-year-old. Not because I think she would be morally corrupted, or become violent or sadistic, but because I'm pretty sure it would be a deeply unpleasant experience.

Also, while content analysis of slasher films has shown that they are not as misogynistic and regressive as rumored,[20] there are slasher films that invite a voyeuristic, sadistic identification with a killer and that linger on sexualized assaults on female characters for no good narrative reason. Such movies should not be banned, if you ask me. People can have perfectly good and ethically defensible reasons for wanting to watch such films—maybe they find them funny in an ironic way, or interesting in a film historical context, or valuable as historical documents, say. Maybe they admire the craftsmanship behind the special effects. When people watch movies, they are not passive receptacles. They engage actively with what they are seeing— process it, interpret it, assess it, maybe resist it. Connoisseurs of trash films, for example, find plenty to enjoy and bond over in such films.[21]

Horror, Violent Media, and Real-World Violence

There is nothing unnatural about being drawn to depictions of violence, even the kind of explicit and realistic violence that is on display in torture porn. As I explained in a previous chapter, humans are biologically disposed to be morbidly curious. Our fascination with the Grim Reaper and his modi operandi is adaptive—a survival mechanism.

Do violent media make us more violent, though? Media psychologists have grappled with that issue for decades, and the consensus seems to be that violent media may be one factor among many in increasing aggressiveness, particularly in individuals prone to violent behavior,[22] although many of the studies finding a link between violent media and aggression have been criticized on methodological grounds.[23] One thing is finding a correlation between use of violent movies and aggressiveness (a correlation that may mean only that aggressive individuals are drawn to violent entertainment), or even a short-term causal relationship in a lab study where subjects are shown a short clip of violence and then asked to fill out a questionnaire about their state of mind. It is something else to get a good fix on a complicated real-world phenomenon.

A team of economists looked at the violent content of blockbuster movies and real-world violence. They found that whenever a violent movie attracted a large audience in movie theaters, violent crime in the United States went *down*.[24] This is probably primarily because would-be perpetrators of violent crime spent the night in a movie theater, rather than getting into drunken trouble on the streets. The researchers concluded that "in the short run, violent movies deter almost 1,000 assaults on an average weekend."[25] Similarly, a study looked at violence in American media in the period 1960–2012 and compared that to the rates of homicide and aggravated assault over the same period.[26] The study found a small negative correlation. Yes, negative. Movie violence went up, real-world violence went down. So it is a little more complicated than "more violent media equals more real-world violence."

For most people, watching the occasional violent, or even ultraviolent, horror movie is unlikely to make a real difference in terms of aggressiveness. There might be better reason to be concerned about those action movies that portray violence slickly, even beautifully, and with no lasting negative consequences for the victims, than the torture porn movies that depict violence in all its grisly horror. And I am not even sure there is reason to be worried about those action films either. Empirical research suggests that exposure to fictional violence does not desensitize even supposedly impressionable young adults to the suffering of real-world victims of violence. They know perfectly well that there is a crucial difference between looking at fictional and real violence.[27]

So, most folks watching violent fictional media, and perhaps especially today's media-literate youth, realize that it is fiction and process it as such. They may find violent entertainment stimulating and exciting, but they engage with it playfully, as simulation, not as an instruction manual to be blindly followed. There is no solid evidence that horror movies corrupt their audience. But just like all other fiction, horror movies may have the power to tweak viewers' moral compass ever so slightly.

Horror and Morality

Horror movies are often moralizing—I mean, they present certain behaviors and characters as good and certain others as bad and have a clear-cut moral agenda. Indeed, they often have a fairly rigid, even Manichaean moral structure. Take *The Exorcist* again. Clearly, the demon Pazuzu and all its harmful actions (including the possession of innocent Regan) are bad, whereas the selfless efforts of the exorcists to banish the demon are good. Or consider Carpenter's *Halloween.* We are encouraged to admire the babysitter character Laurie Strode, who saves the children in her care from the onslaught of Michael Myers, the crazed killer. Conversely, we are invited to pass harsh moral judgment on Myers, who seems to be driven solely by an irrational and immoral desire to harm.

Literary scholars working with social scientists have identified an underlying so-called agonistic structure of fiction: a moral spectrum along which characters are systematically distributed. At one end of that spectrum are protagonists, the good guys; at the other are antagonists, the villains. A fascinating empirical finding in this field is that the motives of antagonists boil down to antisociality. They are selfish, power-hungry, callous individuals. The motives of protagonists, in contrast, boil down to prosociality. They are helpful, other-oriented, self-sacrificing individuals.[28] Indeed, the villains of cinema (including horror's monsters) tend to have selfish motives and to find joy in the infliction of pain on others, as the media researcher Jens Kjeldgaard-Christiansen has shown;[29] they violate all the major moral domains of human conduct.[30]

By immersing ourselves in the imaginative universes of fictional narrative, our moral compasses are subtly adjusted.[31] We thrill when the good guys band together and selflessly take up the fight against terrible adversaries, who are motivated by a selfish striving for power and dominance. The thing is, we all have dispositions for prosocial as well as antisocial behavior; we are perpetually caught in a conflict between getting ahead and getting along. Fiction often dramatizes this conflict and tends to privilege getting along through its agonistic structure.

Consider Stephen King's classic ghost story *The Shining.* The main character, Jack Torrance, is a flawed but likable family man with literary ambitions. Once his family moves into the haunted Overlook Hotel, nefarious supernatural forces in the hotel feed Jack's selfish ambitions and eventually drive him to homicidal madness. His transition from flawed good guy to evil villain is signaled by a shift in his priorities from his family to himself. By the end, he is willing to kill his wife and child in exchange for power and prestige.[32]

A story like *The Shining* reinforces our moral intuitions about the nature of good versus evil. We are reminded that self-sacrificing, other-oriented behavior is good and that selfish, dominance-seeking behavior is bad. But of course, some horror stories are less clear-cut in their moral structure. Some stories present us with morally ambiguous "monsters"—the prototype here is Frankenstein's hapless creature, who is driven to violent aggression through no fault of his own. It is difficult to read Shelley's novel and not feel a measure of sympathy for the monster. A more modern example would be the extraterrestrial creature in J. J. Abrams's 2011 movie *Super 8*. The alien seems to have crash-landed on Planet Earth and has been taken captive by the US Air Force. They treat it as a dangerous monster, when in fact it is just lonely, hungry, and homesick. It takes the empathy and understanding of a bunch of outsider kids (and one outsider scientist) to set the "monster" free. The real monsters in this movie are the narrow-minded, un-empathetic officers who fail to look beyond the extraterrestrial's frightening exterior. *Super 8* urges its viewers to question their own gut reactions, their intuitive moral judgments, and to extend empathy beyond the circle of people who look like them. In this way, horror movies have the ability to encourage introspection and moral reflection.

The tendency of horror movies to moralize is perhaps unsurprising, given the genre's roots in cautionary tales. Such tales vividly depict moral transgressions and the terrible consequences of such transgressions in order to regulate people's behavior. Indeed, some scientists believe that storytelling itself evolved tens or hundreds of thousands of years ago as a cooperation-enhancing mechanism. In contemporary hunter-gatherer societies, those bands that have many skilled storytellers are more cooperative than those bands that have fewer such gifted members.[33] One reason may be that stories are really effective for providing engaging depictions of what happens when people violate social norms, and so the imaginative stories disseminated by skilled storytellers shape listeners' behavior in a prosocial or cooperative direction.

Consider the slasher films that drenched the movie market in the 1980s as an example of a kind of cautionary tale. Many such films depict silly teenagers engaging in activities that, at least from a conservative perspective, are immoral—they have premarital sex, drink alcohol, and do drugs. They are then stalked and killed by a shadowy figure. In *Friday the 13th*, for example, Kevin Bacon's character has sex, smokes weed, and is promptly killed (Fig. 5.2). It looks like cause and effect.

Did the creators of slasher movies set out to convey conservative messages to their audiences? Not necessarily. John Carpenter, the director of *Halloween*, always said that he just wanted to give a realistic depiction of teens. The teenager, in its natural habitat, tends to be interested in sex, alcohol, and drugs. The one teen character to survive in *Halloween*, Laurie Strode, is the one who is not too busy hooking up with guys to pay attention to her surroundings. It is not necessarily that she is a goody two shoes, it is that she stays alert. Also, as the critic and author Les Daniels has wryly pointed out, "Contrary to what casual commentators like to say, sex is not really punished by death in modern horror movies: it only looks like cause and effect

Figure 5.2 In the popular imagination, sex equals death in slasher movies. That's not always the case, but in this scene from Sean S. Cunningham's *Friday the 13th* (Paramount Pictures, 1980), Jack (Kevin Bacon) enjoys a postcoital marijuana cigarette before being murdered by the slasher villain. It certainly looks like cause and effect.

because producers want to show both, and sex before death is more practical."[34]

Stephen King once half-jokingly suggested that horror stories are by their nature deeply conservative:

> The horror story, beneath its fangs and fright-wig, is really as conservative as an Illinois Republican in a three-piece pin-striped suit . . . its main purpose is to reaffirm the virtues of the norm by showing us what awful things happen to people who venture into taboo lands. Within the framework of most horror tales we find a moral code so strong it would make a Puritan smile.[35]

King has a point, but as he would surely acknowledge, it is more complicated than that. As the film critic Robin Wood has pointed out, horror movies can be progressive as well as reactionary.[36] Wood suggested that the ideological orientation of a horror movie can be gleaned from the way in which the monster is depicted. Progressive horror movies invite empathy or even identification with the monster and condemnation of the repressive social forces that produced that monster. An example might be *The Texas Chain Saw Massacre*, in which a group of young people fall prey to a family of laid-off slaughterhouse workers turned cannibalistic. There is here a suggestion that the forces of capitalism can turn against people and devour them. Reactionary horror movies, in contrast, invite condemnation of the monster as pure evil and an affirmation of the social norms that would condemn it. An example would be *The Exorcist*. There are no mitigating circumstances to the demon Pazuzu's behavior; it is simply an evil force that tears good Americans apart.

Where does the so-called rape-revenge film—targeted by Siskel and Ebert in the "women-in-danger" campaign—sit on this ideological spectrum? The rape-revenge film depicts the rape of a female protagonist, followed by an act of retribution carried out against the perpetrators by the victim or her friends or kin. Are such films reactionary and misogynist in their exploitative depictions of sexual violations against attractive female protagonists? Or do they condemn the perpetrators and celebrate the protagonist's vengeful agency?[37] Again, that has to depend on a movie-by-movie analysis, but one thing is certain: the rape-revenge film rouses some mightily powerful emotions.

Like many horror movies, the rape-revenge film evokes moral outrage—and uses moral outrage as a narrative engine—through its depiction of an extreme moral transgression or outright evil. The profoundly unpleasant rape scene is designed to mobilize viewers' condemnation, and the subsequent act of vigilantism—often involving the violated heroine dismembering and killing her assailants—satisfies a deep-seated desire for retribution.[38] That kind of moral setup is not unique to horror, of course. Many a mainstream movie opens with a moral wrong that the protagonist then sets out to right. Take the action movie *John Wick*. An early scene shows bad guys gratuitously killing protagonist John Wick's puppy—a gift from his deceased wife—and stealing his beloved vintage car. It is a minimal setup, but enough to license massive retribution from retired hitman Wick, who ends up killing a whopping 77 opponents during the film.

So horror movies have moral structure and they evoke moral emotions. They encourage us to respond powerfully to depictions of evil acts and creatures, and typically encourage us to take the perspective of those agents of good who take up the fight with the forces of evil. Horror movies can be moralizing, and they can be immoral. But there is nothing immoral about finding pleasure in being frightened by a scary movie, and there is no research to suggest that horror fans are more immoral than non-fans, or that horror movies make people immoral. Rather, horror movies tend to privilege prosocial good over antisocial evil.

Joe Dante—the director of the horror comedy *Gremlins*—explained in an interview how he wanted to convey a political antiwar message with his entry in the *Masters of Horror* television series, "Homecoming," from 2005. "Homecoming" depicted American soldiers fallen in the Iraq War rising from graves to vote in the US presidential election in an attempt to bring an antiwar administration into office. Dante said: "We'd love to make movies that say something, and we love to try to change people's minds, but the fact is that if movies could really change people's minds, we would have all disarmed after *Dr. Strangelove* came out."[39] Dante may have been unduly bleak about horror's potential to "change people's minds," but it seems to be the case that the genre's capacity to influence our values is modest. Horror movies may not make us significantly better people, and they may not make us significantly worse, but they do give a lot of pleasure and meaningful experience to a lot of people.

Those critics who would condemn horror on moral grounds should take a closer look at the genre, watch some of the best movies it has to offer. Otherwise, they risk committing the same error as those shallow villagers who pelted Frankenstein's creature with rocks just because he looked weird. Look beyond form, and you will find that there is a lot of humanity inside.

6

"I'm Nervous That Watching Horror Makes Me Look Stupid"

About five or six years ago, I was invited to a fancy social gathering with the American ambassador to Denmark. I had had some dealings with the US Embassy, which had generously sponsored some educational and research activities in my university department, and so I ended up on a guest list. The invitation came with a dress code ("business casual," a first for me), and the event included movers and shakers from various sectors of Danish professional life. Everybody was very nice.

During self-introductions, I presented myself as a horror researcher. I might as well have farted loudly. There was polite laughter and puzzled smiles. (I can only imagine what would have happened if I had been a porn researcher.) But once I started explaining why horror is a worthwhile research subject, the others seemed genuinely interested and appreciative.

Is there a cultural stigma associated with the horror genre? I think there is, at least in some quarters. It is certainly not as bad as it has been. This is anecdotal, of course, but I have heard stories from horror buffs facing prejudice or even concern for their moral habitus and mental health. Such prejudice seems to have been fairly widespread through the second half of the twentieth century especially. As we have seen, moral panics have accompanied the horror genre with some regularity—in the 1980s, with the video nasties, and in the 1950s, with the horror comics. Many young baby boomers, who had cut their teeth on horror comics such as *Tales from the Crypt* and *Creepy*, were bit by the horror bug with the rise in the late 1950s of "monster culture"[1]—and not always with the approval of their elders.

Mid-century monster culture was largely driven by a renewed fascination with classic Universal Pictures horror movies from the 1930s, such as *Dracula* and *The Mummy*. In the 1950s and 1960s, those movies were broadcast into Americans' homes on the suddenly ubiquitous television set. Monster-happy kids could satisfy their curiosity by getting their hands on newly established fan magazines such as *Famous Monsters of Filmland*, which was edited by now-legendary horror enthusiast Forrest J. Ackerman and which featured movie stills and behind-the-scenes horror movie photographs, and they could buy DIY monster model kits from Aurora Plastics (Fig. 6.1), such as a 12-inch Frankenstein figure. They did so at their own peril, though; many of them faced frowns or worse from concerned adults, who thought that monster fascination was, at best, a waste of time, and at worst a corrupting influence. One of the main characters of Stephen King's 1975 vampire novel, *'Salem's Lot*, is a young boy with a complete collection of Aurora plastic monsters, much to his mother's displeasure. She "thought all that stuff was bad news, rotted your brains or something."[2] Guillermo del Toro, whose first book purchase at the tender age of seven was a copy of *Best Horror Stories* edited by Ackerman, has explained how his childhood love of Universal monsters such as Frankenstein's creature and Count Dracula gave him a lot of pleasure, but also greatly upset his devoutly Catholic family.[3]

In the world of research, almost no academics took horror seriously up until the 1980s. There are exceptions, of course, such as Les Daniels's 1975 book *Living in Fear: A History of Horror in Mass Media*. Nowadays, many horror researchers point to David Punter's trailblazing 1980 book *The Literature of Terror*—which included a chapter on cinematic horror—as a landmark publication that helped to bestow legitimacy on horror as an object of research.[4] Things really took off in the 1990s, though, with the rise of cultural studies and the emerging legitimacy of studying even popular culture.

Nowadays, there are professional organizations for horror scholars, dedicated academic journals, horror conferences, and so on. Things have changed, but it seems like horror is still viewed, at least by some, as a fairly dumb genre—shallow or even

Figure 6.1 The classic 1930s monster movies from Universal Studios, such as *Dracula* (directed by Tod Browning, 1931) and *Frankenstein* (directed by James Whale, 1931), got second wind when they were broadcast on television in the 1950s and 1960s and gave rise to "monster culture." Many American kids were crazy for the new DIY plastic monster models from Aurora Plastics in the early 1960s. This full-page monster model ad was featured in *Boy's Life*, the magazine of the Boy Scouts of America, in the October 1962 issue.

mind-numbing popular entertainment that speaks to "primitive" emotion rather than the intellect. Yes, the horror genre does take its name from an emotion, and emotion is crucial to the horror movie, as we have seen. But horror movies can also tickle the intellect—and I don't see why emotional stimulation should be less valuable than intellectual stimulation anyway.

One symptom of the stigma that attaches to horror is the fact that horror movies rarely get prestigious accolades, such as Academy Awards. Only one horror movie has gotten the coveted Academy Award for Best Picture, and that was *The Silence of the Lambs* back in 1992. To complicate the matter, the generic classification of that movie has been fiercely contested, with both critics and fans arguing over whether it is a horror movie or a thriller or a drama or a mystery film.[5] Then there is the South Korean *Parasite*, which won for Best Picture in 2019. That movie has some horror elements, such as an eerie ghost and some pretty gory homicides,[6] but it is not usually described as horror. So, for a bona fide horror movie to get an Oscar in the Best Picture category is a rarity, even though such movies are occasionally nominated in the category: *The Exorcist* in 1973, *Jaws* in 1975, *The Sixth Sense* in 1999, *District 9* in 2009, *Black Swan* in 2010, and *Get Out* in 2017.

So if you are concerned about your cultural capital, you are probably better off quoting Shakespeare or Dickinson at a cocktail party (or an English department staff meeting) than lines from horror movies. But why would horror have that stigma? Well, the subjects of horror are not necessarily fit for polite company. "Hi, nice to meet you too. What I'm currently working on? Uh, demonic possession, ritual sacrifice, flesh-eating ghouls, chainsaw killers, extra-dimensional abominations, that sort of thing." Also, some people associate the genre with cheap and unsophisticated tricks—profit-hungry filmmakers dishing out jump scares and gory imagery.

Historically, horror fans have occasionally been seen as brutish thrill-seekers looking for a cheap kick or hoping to satisfy their perverse desire to look at broken bodies.[7] As the media scholar David Buckingham has noted (writing in the early 1990s), "Perhaps to a greater extent than any other group of fans, horror enthusiasts are stigmatised from all sides."[8] And often, when a horror movie gets critical success, it is called something other than horror. Jordan Peele's 2017 hit *Get Out*, for example, very self-consciously used horror and sci-fi cinematic conventions to tell its story about racial oppression, but critics were quick to call it a "social thriller," I guess because that sounds more respectable. And in the wake of a crop of artistically ambitious, occasionally convention-bending horror flicks in the 2010s, journalists started throwing around terms like "post-horror" and "elevated horror" and *really* annoyed a lot of horror connoisseurs.

"Post-Horror" and "Elevated Horror"

Some people felt that horror was going in circles in the 2000s, with an endless stream of remakes, reboots, sequels, and prequels.[9] That is not quite fair, because that decade did see some truly excellent horror movies, such as *Cloverfield* and *Drag Me to Hell*. But things did get particularly exciting in the 2010s—exciting enough for some film reviewers to start talking about a horror renaissance, a new Golden Age of American Horror Movies, the likes of which had not been seen since the 1970s. New visionary, horror-happy production companies cropped up, such as Blumhouse Productions and A24, and the golden age was heralded by aesthetically ambitious, genre-savvy horror movies like *It Follows*, *The VVitch*, *A Quiet Place*, *It Comes at Night*, *Get Out*, and *Hereditary*. The first instalment in Andy Muschietti's two-movie adaptation of Stephen King's killer-clown classic *It* came out in 2017 and broke all box-office records for horror. That film was fairly conventional, but it did feature A-list actors and had a stunning production design.

So what was happening? Was horror reinventing or even transcending itself (whatever that would mean)? The freelance cinema writer Steve Rose suggested in a 2017 article in *The Guardian* that something truly novel was happening.[10] He said that "a new breed of horror is creeping into the multiplex, replacing jump scares with existential dread." Rose's term for this "new breed" was "post-horror." His article was inspired in part by the divided reception of *It Comes at Night*, a low-budget, post-apocalyptic, and fairly "artsy" horror movie, which was admired by critics but less so by horror buffs. Rose's article became a lightning rod for irate connoisseurs, who pointed out that horror movies have *always* been willing to engage with existential dread and the "big, metaphysical questions" that Rose said was the province of "post-horror."

Other journalists embraced the term "elevated horror," which was often used in connection with Ari Aster's 2018 supernatural family drama *Hereditary*,[11] but which seems to have been in use since 2010.[12] In December 2019, the magazine *Esquire* published an article with the title "The 2010s Were the Decade When Horror Got Smart."[13] The writer, Tom Nicholson, discussed some of the "elevated" horror films I have mentioned (as well as the independent 2014 Australian movie *The Babadook*), and said that what "really connects those films . . . is their smartness. They're brilliant, entertaining, thought-provoking films, which have not historically been the kind of adjectives associated with the genre." That is all true, but you can see why connoisseurs were upset with these news stories that claimed that horror was transcending itself. They did not feel that there was anything that needed transcending. To them, "smart horror" had never been an oxymoron.

Terms like "post-horror" and "elevated horror" seem to imply that traditional horror is inferior to this new stuff, and that the new stuff is good *because* it transcends genre, or surpasses traditional horror (or "low horror," I guess). But what is "post" or "elevated" about it? Is it that this new horror is socially conscious, like *Get Out*? Well, we have had socially conscious horror movies for a very long time—Romero's 1968 movie *Night of the Living Dead*, say, which tackled social disintegration in the guise of an apocalyptic zombie outbreak. Is it the focus on psychological states, the depiction of complex characters? That is nothing new, either. Norman Bates from Hitchcock's *Psycho* (1960) is a pretty complex character. The focus on existential themes? That stuff goes way back, to *Frankenstein* and beyond. Is it the fact that these new movies are aesthetically ambitious? Well, so was

The Shining from 1980 and *Rosemary's Baby* from 1968—and *Nosferatu* from 1922, for that matter. Is it that these new films seem to use the elements of horror not as a goal in themselves, but as a means to an end, such as the exploration of pathological family relationships or existential themes? If so, horror movies have done that for a long time.

I am not at all convinced that there is anything truly new about these horror movies from the 2010s, apart from their acclaim, but as a horror fan I am thrilled to be finding myself in the midst of a deluge of really good horror movies. If nothing else, these movies may help reduce genre stigma and prejudice. Maybe more mainstream production companies will see that horror is no obstacle to quality (or revenue); maybe more first-rate directors and actors will be attracted to the genre; maybe more critics will open-mindedly approach movies with a horror label; maybe funding agencies will become more willing to invest money in genre movies. And maybe, eventually, you will not have to worry about looking stupid when you are buying tickets to a horror movie.

Critics versus Audiences

For now, though, some stigma seems to remain. And while horror movies certainly can be intelligent, it is perhaps no coincidence that horror "has been the worst reviewed genre amongst all movies with relative consistency," according to the movie analyst Stephen Follows.[14] Maybe horror movies have a peculiar ratio of good to bad. The science fiction writer Theodore Sturgeon once got tired of people always disrespecting sci-fi. He said, sure, 90% of science fiction is crud—but 90% of *everything* is crud, and let us focus on the good 10%.[15] (This has come to be known as Sturgeon's Law.) Maybe for horror, it is 92% or even 93%. Many more horror movies are produced today than ever before, as we have seen, but the proportion of truly excellent horror movies may be constant, so that the absolute number of excellent horror movies is increasing. That would mean that excellent horror movies become more visible, which may help explain the at least partly misguided gushing over "post-horror" and "elevated horror."

Interestingly, there is an extremely low correlation between film critics' rating of a horror film and its profitability. For all other genres, the correlation hovers between .8 and 1.[16] That means that if critics like a non-horror film, there is a very high likelihood of that film making good money. What is the correlation between critics' rating of a horror film and its profitability? Take a guess. In the meantime, let me give a basic introduction to correlation coefficients. Correlation coefficients go from -1 to 1, and they indicate the relationship between two variables. The closer to 1 a correlation is, the more positively associated the two variables are. For example, outdoor temperature and ice cream sales would probably have a correlation coefficient close to 1. One goes up, so does the other. 0 means no correlation, like the relationship between how many cups of coffee you drink in a given year and automobile sales in your country, and -1 is a perfect negative correlation. An example of a negative correlation would be outdoor temperature and parka sales. Now, if you are looking to predict the profitability of a horror movie by investigating critics' ratings of it, you might as well try to predict annual automobile sales by counting how many cups of coffee you drink—well, almost. The correlation between critics' ratings of horror movies and their profitability is .17.

Why is that? It could be that critics are out of sync. What they like may not be what audiences like (in the domain of horror, at least). It could also be that horror movies have appeals that fall outside critical criteria of quality. Evidently, some horror movies that are not very good by traditional critical standards still attract large audiences—teenagers looking for a night of fun thrills, say. For some, a movie full of effective jump scares but with crudely drawn characters, stilted dialogue, and gaping plot holes may still be a satisfying horror movie, if what they are looking for is a fright, a jolt to the nervous system. So it could very well be the case that there are bigger audiences for bad horror movies than there are for bad dramas, say, or bad action films.

Take the 2014 audience hit *Annabelle*, a prequel to *The Conjuring* and the first in a whole series of films about a possessed doll. It was made for a measly $6.5 million. Critics did not like it. On Metacritic. com, a website that compiles reviews, *Annabelle* has a weighted average score of 37 out of 100, which translates to "generally unfavorable reviews,"[17] which is a polite way of saying that critics thought it sucked. I am with the critics here—I did not think it was very good. But it did make a *lot* of money—$257 million in global box office. That is a very impressive return on investment. Maybe, despite being generously panned by critics, the film fulfilled some need for at least some audiences. Or maybe they were all just duped into watching it by successful marketing, although I doubt it. Word of mouth travels fast. And to be fair, I had a lot of fun watching and critiquing it with my wife and kids.

Snobbery, Education, and Horror

There may still be some snobbish prejudice toward horror, and it does look like horror movies may be slightly more popular with people of relatively low socioeconomic status. In our big study on horror and personality, we found a small negative correlation between horror liking and educational attainment among our American respondents.[18] In other words, the better educated people are, the less likely they are to be horror fans. Similarly, Stephen Follows found that in the United Kingdom, horror movies are seen by a slightly higher proportion of working-class and non-working people than are other genres.[19] Why? We do not know, but one explanation is that cultural elites still frown on horror as a fairly unsavory aspect of popular culture. If you are well educated and roam in well-educated circles, you may find yourself surrounded by people who look down on horror—people who can quote Shakespeare and Dickinson, but who would not know George Romero from John Carpenter.

If that is the case, it is a bit ironic. Horror cinema has its roots in an ancient narrative tradition with an impressive literary pedigree. The anglophone literary tradition really is peppered with the elements of horror. If you want a scary story with witches and creepy visions and ghosts, you could do a lot worse than Shakespeare's *Macbeth*. And Emily Dickinson gravitated toward some mightily dark material in her poetry. One of her poems begins, "I heard a fly buzz—when I died" . . . and it just gets darker from there.

Horror movies can be smart and challenging and complex and all the rest. There is nothing about the genre that makes it inherently dumb—inappropriate as a subject for dinner party patter, maybe, but not dumb. And as I have mentioned before (but am pleased to mention again), horror viewers are not passive receptacles; they engage actively and sometimes critically with what they watch. They respond to the aesthetic qualities of movies. As del Toro says: "We have to admit and enshrine the fact that this is a genre that has given us some of the most indelible images in the history of cinema."[20] Horror buffs talk about the beautiful dolly shot in *Texas Chain Saw Massacre* where the camera ominously tracks a character walking toward a creepy house. They talk about the clockwork choreography of the big scene in *Halloween* where the main character discovers the corpses of her friends, one after another, in a crescendo of terror. They enjoy the clever play with genre convention in *Cabin in the Woods* (Fig. 6.2), the painstakingly controlled mise-en-scène in *The Shining*, and the excellent acting in *Drag Me to Hell*. They are still up against some prejudice, it seems, but much less than has historically been the case.

Literally Looking Stupid

There is another kind of nervous would-be horror viewer that we need to talk about before we move on to the next subject, and that is the person who is afraid of looking stupid—literally. The person who is utterly unconcerned about cultural capital and genre hierarchies and all of that stuff, but who is afraid of being laughed at when they respond powerfully to a horror movie by shrieking or jumping in the seat.

I have a friend and colleague who is like that. I will not name him, because I know it bothers him, but he will startle and yell when there

Figure 6.2 Horror movies aren't necessarily as dumb as their reputation would suggest. *The Cabin in the Woods* (Lionsgate, directed by Drew Goddard, 2011), for example, is chock-full of clever play with genre convention, as in this shot which riffs on countless careless-youths-arrive-at-secluded-cabin-in-the-woods-and-very-bad-things-happen movies.

is a solid jump scare. I mean, startle like a jumping jack on meth and yell to make your eardrums hum. He is a big guy, jacked. He could knock somebody out, jumping like that. There is a technical term for such a person that I mentioned in Chapter 2—a "hyperstartler."[21] A hyperstartler responds much more strongly to a startle cue than the rest of us. Scientists do not yet know why some people are hyperstartlers, whether it is in their upbringing or genes.[22] But such individuals are often the butt of startle jokes. Jokesters will enjoy sneaking up on them and eliciting a powerful response with a simple cue.

Watching a horror movie with a hyperstartler can be fun, but even watching a horror movie with somebody whose startle system is not overclocked can be amusing. There is a peculiar pleasure in seeing somebody else respond powerfully to a basically innocuous cue—respond as if they are in acute, life-threatening danger even though they are just looking at patterns of light on a two-dimensional screen and listening to artificial sounds.

Humor researchers have uncovered the underlying structure of what we find funny, and most funny things can be reduced to *benign violations*.[23] We tend to find things funny when they have those two qualities: benignity, that is, the quality of being non-threatening; and involving a violation of some kind—a break with one's beliefs about normality and propriety. Now, when people scream because of a jump scare, they are acting as if there was actual danger. There is not, of course, and that is the violation. They are violating an expectation that a fearful response follows a fearsome stimulus. But the violation is benign, there is no harm done. So it is funny.

I have mentioned previously the research we have been doing in a Danish haunted house. Usually, after a night of data collection, I will stick around for the debrief. That is when all the volunteers—actors, technicians, builders, guards, caterers, makeup artists, and so on—gather to hear from the organizers about how the night's haunt has gone. They will get information about guest feedback, security issues, changes in the set design, that sort of thing. After the debrief, the volunteers have something to drink and almost invariably start swapping stories about guest behavior, laughing uproariously at stories about guests overreacting. A scare actor will tell a story about a guest wetting themselves in terror to a group of other actors, who will be laughing and nodding appreciatively, acknowledging the actor's craftsmanship.

In 2019, we mounted surveillance cameras in several rooms within the haunt. One night, after debrief, an actor told me to check out the footage from her room. I did. What I saw was a rundown room with an old couch in the middle. A dead-looking woman sits on the couch. Four teenage girls enter the room. They wander around a bit, trying to figure out what to do. The deadish woman stays stock-still. Then two of the girls sit down on the couch, one on each side of the actor. And then the actor reaches out for one of the girls, who has such a fright that she screams piercingly, topples over the armrest, does a backward somersault, and lands on all fours on the floor (Fig. 6.3).

The girl is okay—she jumps right back onto her feet and straightens her hair—but her friends are laughing like maniacs, and the actor is obviously having a very hard time keeping a straight face. Now, the girl knew that she was in a haunted house attraction and that the dead-looking woman on the couch was an actor in makeup, but a

Figure 6.3 Because of the stigma that still clings to the horror genre, its fans are sometimes worried about looking stupid. And sometimes they *do* look a little, uh, unfortunate, as in this surveillance image from a commercial haunted house where a startled guest jumps in fright and falls off a couch. Apart from suffering the pain of being laughed at by her friends, the guest did not get hurt. Photo courtesy of the author.

powerful startle response still overrode all that rational knowledge. You are supposed to be frightened in a haunted house, but not *that* frightened. The girl's behavior violated everybody's expectations, but in a benign way (because she did not suffer anything worse than transitory embarrassment). So it was funny.

So, if your concern is looking stupid when you scream and jump or just stare at the screen with bulging eyes, I am afraid there is little you can do. Maybe you can find some solace in the fact that you will be providing amusement to your co-viewers. And if they give you a hard time, just tell them that at least your fear system is in excellent shape—you are a natural-born survivor.

7

"I'm Nervous about Kids Watching Horror"

Here are two scenes from my childhood. Scene 1: A couple of detectives pull over a car. They arrest the driver and open the trunk of the car. Inside the trunk is a dead person. The dead person has a sickly green pallor and wide-open, milky eyes. Scene 2: A lonely hut is visible on an icy, arctic plain. A huge, human-like figure emerges from behind the hut and shambles toward the entrance. The figure— a hulking monstrosity—is overgrown with some kind of green fungus.

They are, of course, scenes from movies that I watched. I do not remember anything else from those movies, and I do not remember how old I was, but those two scenes frightened me badly, and they stayed with me.

I am certainly not alone in having such vivid memories of being frightened by movies in childhood. There is a whole website called Kindertrauma about "the movies, books, and toys that scared you when you were a kid." The website gleefully solicits "Traumafessions"—personal anecdotes from users about things (usually movies) that terrified them as kids. And media psychologists have demonstrated that such memories are close to a cultural universal.[1] Almost everybody has a memory of some movie or television show that scared them badly, and as I have mentioned, lots of people have suffered from nightmares and minor behavioral disturbances, such as feeling compelled to sleep with the lights on or checking for monsters underneath the bed before going to sleep. Media researchers have consequently expressed great concerns over the effects of scary movies on children especially.[2]

Here is another scene, but this one is from real life: my daughter, Laura, is at the dentist. She is about 10 years old and high on laughing gas—she is having a permanent tooth extracted. About a year before, she had been pestering her mom and me to take her to a commercial haunted house. The haunted house in question, Dystopia Haunted House, does not normally allow entry for people under the age of 13, but I know the owners, as I have been consulting for them for a while. I can probably get special permission. It is a bit of a dilemma, though. We are thinking that if we do take her with us on a tour of the haunted house, things can go one of two ways: either she has a really, truly bad time of it, perhaps with nightmares and minor behavioral disturbances to follow, *or* she has a great time, an experience of having successfully challenged herself and mastered her own fear. In the end we figure it is worth the gamble—she is a robust girl, and we have had fun watching some fairly frightening movies together, like *Jaws* and *Jurassic Park*—and so we go through the haunted house.

We are, of course, all of us terrified. We dread whatever is coming up as we are feeling our way along dark hallways, small clammy hands grasped in bigger, equally clammy ones, and we jump in startled synchrony at all the scares. But we are also having a lot of fun, and on the whole, it is a resounding success—a bonding experience, one to which we keep returning in conversations. So, fast-forward to that dentist visit. Laura is lying in the chair, the dentists are working their dark magic, there is a lot of blood. One of the dentists asks Laura if she is okay, if she can handle it. She rolls her eyes in highly accomplished preteen style and says, "I made it through Dystopia. I think I can handle this."

As these anecdotes suggest, horror can have both negative and positive effects on young people. But while there has been a *lot* of research on the negative effects of horror movies on children and adolescents,[3] there has been almost no research on the benefits—same as with the potential mental health benefits that I talked about in an earlier chapter. As the media effects specialist Barbara J. Wilson—who has done her share of research into the negative effects of frightening media—has put it, "So much public attention has been paid to potential negative effects of the media on children that parents and researchers alike have scarcely acknowledged the positive."[4]

I am sure all that research on negative effects comes from a good place—from a combination of scientific curiosity and genuine concern—but it is often quite one-eyed. One influential research article from 1999 asked college students about their memories of encounters with frightening media.[5] Students were asked to recall "a movie that frightened you when you were younger (a child or teen)." They were then asked about their behavior during the film, and about aftereffects. The questionnaire items about behavior during the film included "I was shaking," "I was crying/yelling/screaming," and "My heart was beating fast." The items about effects experienced after the film included "general sense of fear or anxiety, nervous, jumpy, looking over your shoulder" and "fear of sleeping alone." After summing up the results of their study, the authors concluded that "most people have seen a movie that has terrified them and can report a variety of negative effects from seeing that movie." Yes, most people have experienced negative effects, but I would guess that most people would also have positive memories about good times with horror movies. Yet if researchers ask only about negative effects and bad memories, that is what they will get.

It is hardly surprising, then, that the authors of this particular study (like many researchers in the media-effects tradition) seem puzzled about the appeal of scary movies. In response to their own question about "what makes these movies so popular and financially successful," they write: "Perhaps enjoyment stems from a general . . . mastery of fear, or humor and enjoyment derived from the predictability of the script of such films, such as in the recent film *Scream*, which was a scary movie about a group of friends watching scary movies." It is not much of an explanation. Mastery of fear, sure, that sounds plausible, if fairly vague. But humor and enjoyment derived from the predictability of horror films? Yes, one can adopt an ironic viewing stance toward really crappy horror movies, as I have mentioned before, but I do not think that young viewers find themselves drawn toward scary movies in eager anticipation of reflexive meta-viewing. They are not in it to have a knowing laugh at overused genre conventions. No, they are morbidly curious about this dark and forbidden stuff.

Also, *Scream* was successful in part because it was unpredictable—an intelligent twist on well-established genre conventions. It was not about "a group of friends watching scary movies," any more than *Casablanca* is about a guy playing the piano. Yes, there is a scene in *Scream* where a bunch of people are watching *Halloween*, but one wonders whether these researchers have even seen the movie. You would think that a deep knowledge of horror would be a real asset if you were trying to scientifically research the psychology behind the genre, but it is far from always the case that media psychologists who study fright reactions to scary movies have such knowledge, and I think that is partly why such research is biased toward negative effects. For an outsider, the horror genre probably appears formulaic and stupid, if not downright morally objectionable. For many children, however, scary stories have an undeniable allure.

Children and Horror

Kids seem to be naturally drawn to frightening stories, whether on screen or paper. They are fascinated with monsters and intrigued by scary tales. There is a reason why the ghost story told around the camp bonfire is such a cliché. A large-scale British survey of school children's reading habits from 2005, involving more than 8,000 children, asked about kids' fiction preferences. Guess how many indicated "horror/ghost stories" as a favorite type of fiction? A whopping 53%.[6] And the media scholar David Buckingham conducted a series of in-depth interviews with children (ranging from six to 16 years of age) and their families about emotional responses to television. He found that horror was popular "across the whole range" of his sample—and that children enjoyed talking about their experiences with horror.[7]

An older study, published in 1983, recruited 43 second-grade kids and 46 sixth-grade kids and asked them (through a questionnaire) about their relationship with scary television. One question was: "How much do you like scary television programs?" Among the young children, 36% said "a lot" and 28% "not at all." Among the older children, 41% said "a lot" and only 7% said "not at all."[8] This research supports other previously mentioned studies that have found that the appetite for horror media increases during childhood, peaks in adolescence, and gradually decreases for the rest of one's life.[9]

Now, most of the research on children's engagement with and psychological responses to horror focuses on movies intended for adult or teenaged audiences. *The Exorcist* was never intended for kids, nor was *Jaws*. As the film scholar Catherine Lester puts it, children's horror seems to be an "impossible subgenre."[10] Horror movies are supposed to scare their audience, but we are not supposed to scare kids too badly . . . so if a horror movie for kids drastically tones down the scary material to avoid traumatizing young viewers, is it still a horror movie? Yes—to a kid, anyway. So children's horror is not, after all, an oxymoron—and there is a cinematic subgenre of children's horror movies, such as the 1987 cult movie *The Monster Squad*, just as there are horror-themed television shows for kids, such as *Scooby-Doo*. And as Lester has pointed out, there are plenty of children's movies and television series that include scary material, not least such quintessentially wholesome family entertainment as the Disney classics. Who can forget Snow White's frenzied flight through the haunted forest in the Disney classic from 1937?

Since the 1980s, an increasing number of movies have combined horror and comedy and attracted a lot of young viewers—*Gremlins*, for instance, and *Ghostbusters*. *Gremlins* had received a PG rating ("Parental Guidance Suggested"), but its dark content disturbed some people and the public controversy over the appropriateness of the movie for kids led to the addition of the PG-13 rating ("Parents Strongly Cautioned") in the Motion Picture Association of America's rating system.[11] This may actually have been a good thing for children's horror, since "it opened further space to create horror films that were not too intense or violent to be given a restrictive rating but were frightening enough that extra warning would be needed to indicate that the films might distress young children," as Lester says.[12]

Lately, we have seen quite a few children's films with horror content, such as *Coraline* from 2009, *ParaNorman* from 2012, and the *Hotel Transylvania* series (with three movies so far—one from 2012, one from 2015, and one from 2018). You will find uncanny doppelgängers, decomposing zombies, and bloodthirsty vampires in those movies, but they characteristically use distancing techniques to avoid upsetting their young target audience too much. All these movies are animated, to clearly signal unreality, and they all have happy endings. They also all contain plenty of comedy to mitigate episodes of suspense and horror. In *ParaNorman*, for instance, the protagonist, Norman, can see and talk to dead people and animals. In one scene, Norman's friend Neil asks if Norman can communicate with Neil's dead dog, which was run over by a truck. The ghost dog materializes in front of Norman, but it is cut in half across the middle, divided into two parts. That is pretty grisly. But then, the front part runs behind the back part—the ghost dog sniffs its own butt. That is pretty funny, and takes the sting off the horror of a dismembered family dog from beyond the grave. Also, the decomposing zombies of *ParaNorman* look fairly goofy—they are hardly the stuff of nightmares (Fig. 7.1).

With the rise of children's horror, it seems that we are becoming more tolerant of children's appetite for scary make-believe. You only have to go back a few decades to find pundits—including respectable psychologists—publicly expressing deep concerns about kids becoming satanists and murderers because of Dungeons & Dragons, slasher movies, and live role-playing.

Nowadays, we know much more about the importance of pretend play to psychological and social well-being as well as cognitive aptitude,[13] and about the naturalness of kids' fascination with monsters and scary stories. Children tend to enjoy playful activities that allow them to flirt with fear, such as chase play or hide-and-seek.[14] Such activities allow them to immerse themselves in threat simulations and to acquaint themselves with the darker areas of the emotional spectrum. What does it feel like to be afraid? To be anxious? How much fear can I handle? How can I regulate my own emotions? Children can learn about the world—the inner world as well as the

Figure 7.1 Horror movies for children will use a variety of techniques to alleviate the emotional impact of frightening material on young viewers. Such movies are often animated (to clearly signal unreality), for instance, and often depict monsters that are more dopey than dreadful, as in this depiction of goofy zombies from the PG-rated stop-motion animated horror movie *ParaNorman* (Laika, directed by Sam Fell and Chris Butler, 2012).

outer one—both through playful enactments of threat scenarios and through scary stories. The trick is to avoid overwhelming or even traumatizing them. I once saw a meme consisting of a photo of a cute but worried-looking baby. The caption: "Played peek-a-boo today. Does Mommy think abandonment is funny?" Well, no, probably she does not. But most mothers—and caretakers in general— instinctively realize that kids tend to find great pleasure in mild threat simulations. You do not want to watch *Pet Sematary* with a nine-year-old, but you might consider the shared thrills offered by something like *Hotel Transylvania*.

Children's Fears

Childhood is a time of wild fears and grueling anxieties. Kids are afraid of so much, from the realistic to the wildly implausible—from falling down a flight of stairs to being flayed, cooked, and eaten by an evil witch. They fear getting hurt, being abandoned, being ostracized, being ridiculed, being assaulted, dying. They fear isolation and the dark. Wild animals. Basements. Lonely woods. Even innocuous things can scare kids.

There was a painting on the wall in my childhood home. It was a portrait of a woman in profile (*Annette*, by the Danish artist Kurt Trampedach). Boy, I dreaded passing that picture alone at night—and I had to pass it on my way to the bathroom. The woman in the picture is pale and has a mane of black hair. There is something wild about that hair, but she looks serene, focused. Now, that painting is not supposed to be frightening or even unsettling, I don't think, and looking at it today, online, I find it atmospheric and suggestive—not at all creepy. But how it terrified me. I was deeply worried that as I was passing by, the woman in the painting would turn her head and fix me with those inscrutable, intense eyes. I knew that could not happen, but the *what if* was enough to send me into a barely controlled panic every time I passed that painting alone. The power of the *what if* is very, very strong with children.

As children grow up, their fears change systematically. It is not that they gradually become fearless; the old fears recede into the background and new ones emerge. An infant is afraid of abandonment and strangers. Once it starts moving about on its own, it becomes afraid of heights. When it reaches about four years of age, the child starts fearing wild animals, monsters, and death. Then, in middle to late childhood, fears of injury, accidents, and contagion take center stage. In late childhood and early adolescence, social fears become particularly salient.[15] A preteen would probably rather face an evil witch than peer ridicule and social exclusion.

At a more general level, researchers have found that young children tend to respond more strongly to perceptual qualities (such as distorted faces), whereas older children respond more strongly to conceptual or abstract qualities (such as mean-spiritedness).[16] Things that look scary freak out small kids. Take those two examples I mentioned in the beginning of the chapter. The corpse freaked me out, and so did that arctic fungus creature. For all I know today, perhaps the fungus creature was in fact a kind-hearted soldier in a ghillie suit, out to rescue stranded arctic explorers. But tiny me did not find his motivations or his character important—he looked scary, that was all that mattered.

The media researchers Cynthia Hoffner and Joanne Cantor conducted a fascinating study back in the 1980s to get a better understanding of developmental differences in fright reactions to scary media.[17] The setup was simple but ingenious. The researchers produced a short, animated film, in which two children enter an old woman's house in search of their lost dog. They hear the old woman's voice and hide under a table. The old woman then discovers a stray cat in her house. Here is the twist: there are four versions of the film. In one version, the old woman is a kind-looking, grandmotherly figure who coddles the stray cat and gives it cream. In another, she is also kind-looking but mean, throwing the cat down the basement stairs and saying she will starve it. Then there is a version in which the old woman is an ugly, grotesque witch who is mean to the cat— and a version in which she is a witch who is kind to the cat. In all four versions, the film stops before the old woman discovers the children hiding under her table.

The researchers recruited a bunch of kids in different age groups: three- to five-year-olds, six- to seven-year-olds, and nine- to 10-year-olds, about 50 from each group. They were shown different versions of the film and asked to rate the old woman on a scale from nice to mean. The young children "tended to think the woman was nice when she was attractive and mean when she was ugly"—they relied on appearance rather than behavior in their moral evaluation of the character. The older children, in contrast, put less stock on her appearance and more on her behavior.[18] If she acted kindly, they figured, she must be kind, even if she looked conventionally evil. The children were also asked to predict how the woman would react when she discovered the kids in the film. The young children thought the ugly woman—whether she had behaved kindly or cruelly toward the stray cat—would lock the kids in a closet, whereas the older children did not base their predictions on appearance, but on behavior.

Children's media often tap into this childish tendency to conflate moral ugliness with physical ugliness (and other forms of morally irrelevant deviation from an idealized norm). In older Disney movies, for instance, it is generally quite easy to spot the villains—often on their exterior alone. They look unappealing, and they often have a non-standard-American accent. Take Maleficent from *Sleeping Beauty*, with her yellow eyes and grayish skin, or the morbidly obese Ursula from *The Little Mermaid*, or British-speaking Scar from *The Lion King*. They are all quite clearly "othered," to use a bit of critical jargon. Recently, though, Disney villains have become much harder to spot.[19] The corporation has been avoiding this suspect conflation of unattractiveness with immorality, probably to avoid ideological backlash. For instance, who would have thought that physically appealing and apparently gentlemanly Hans of *Frozen* was the bad guy?

So children are afraid of many different things, and their fears change fairly predictably during development. Children's fears range from very real threats to utterly implausible dangers, and as they mature, children's fears gradually become more abstract, but they often retain their infantile fears of monsters and darkness. Kids can be deeply frightened by the fantasy threats of animated movies—but can they not tell it is just fiction? Are they really as unskilled in the art of distinguishing fantasy from reality as rumor (and some child psychologists) would have it?

Children do seem to have a harder time making a clear distinction between reality and fantasy than adults do, but some research suggests that they may actually be better at making that distinction than many people think. (Besides, adults also sometimes conflate fantasy and reality, and the frightening eruption of fantasy into reality, as well as the inability to tell the two apart, are such common fears that they are active themes in many horror movies. Take the protagonist in *Rosemary's Baby*, who cannot tell whether she is paranoid or whether a coven of evil, black-magic-wielding witches is out to get her baby.) Indeed, even five-year-olds understand that what they are watching is fiction and not real; they may actually have a bias for overgeneralizing, supposing that *everything* on television is fiction.[20] So fantasy and reality are not interchangeable in children's minds. However, realizing that something is fantasy—make-believe—does not necessarily render it completely harmless or inconsequential to a child.

A fascinating study, published in 1991, set out to probe children's capacity for distinguishing between reality and fantasy.[21] The researchers noted that even four-year-olds were quite good at distinguishing between real items and imagined ones. Here is the cool part, though. The research team invited children (four- and six-year-olds) into a room one by one. In this room, besides the experimenter, were two big black boxes, each about three feet by three feet. There was a small hole, about half an inch in diameter, in each box. There was also a stick, about a foot long. The kids were then asked to imagine that there was a "little, friendly puppy" in one box and a "big, scary monster" in the other. They were asked to pretend that if they put their finger into the hole in the puppy box, the dog would lick their finger, but if they put their finger in the monster box hole, the monster would bite their finger clean off. Now, the kids realized that both the puppy and the monster were pretend, not real. But when they were invited to stick their fingers in the holes, many of the kids weren't so happy about poking the monster box—they would rather use the stick, or stay clear of that box altogether.

So children do distinguish between fantasy and reality, and they do realize that something that exists in their imagination (or on a screen) may not exist in the external world.[22] But their imagination is leaky. The monsters that are born there easily seep into the child's perceived external world. Consciously or not, the children in the monster-in-a-box study were probably operating on a "better safe than sorry" principle. As I said before, *what if* thinking is mighty powerful with children.

Can Horror Be Good for Kids?

Children are naturally drawn to scary stories, but they are also easily overwhelmed by such stories, especially in audiovisual media—movies and videogames—that feed them powerful images supported by frightening sounds. However, children can also have positive and empowering experiences with such stories, as my anecdote with the haunted house suggests, even though such experiences have largely been overlooked by horror researchers so far. Children can use frightening stories to learn about themselves and the world and to probe and challenge their own boundaries. They can have intensely gratifying social experiences with horror. As Buckingham shows in his interview study, the social dimension of horror-watching really is crucial to children.

Horror movies might even serve as a kind of stress inoculation for young people. Now, this is purely speculative, but there is research to suggest that moderate adversity early in life might actually enhance resilience and overall well-being.[23] The "moderate" is crucial here: too much adversity is detrimental, but perhaps surprisingly, so is no adversity at all. This kind of research is correlational, meaning that researchers will look into people's life history and also their current mental health and well-being, and look for statistical relationships. You cannot very well do an experimental study on such questions—I mean, you cannot take a bunch of kids and make them miserable for a few weeks, and then see if they handle stress better when they are young adults. But scientists have done that sort of thing with nonhuman primates.

Researchers have been interested in so-called stress inoculation in spider monkeys. They are little tree-dwelling monkeys from Central and South America (with very long limbs, hence the name). In one study, researchers exposed baby spider monkeys to various levels of stress (for instance by separating them from their moms for a short period of time).[24] Ten weeks after those stress trials, the babies would be taken to a new cage with their moms and researchers would observe their behaviors and measure the levels of stress hormone in their blood. Intriguingly, those monkey babies that had been exposed to moderate stress early in life were less likely to cling to their moms in this new environment and started to explore it more quickly, and had less stress hormone in their blood. The ones that had not been stressed at all, as well as the ones that had been exposed to a lot of stress, were more fearful.

Human kids are not that different from spider monkeys, and a similar principle might apply. Moderate stress exposure may have an inoculating effect. Kids need to learn what it feels like to be a little afraid, a little anxious; they need to learn coping strategies for negative emotion. It could very well be the case that scary stories *in moderation* is an effective inoculum. The coping competence developed through engagement with scary media might help them not only in future encounters with such media, but with life itself. Nobody goes through life without having to tackle some fear, some anxiety, some dread.

What Can You Do?

If you want to protect a child from the negative effects that media psychologists have so carefully documented, the most effective course of action would be total media abstinence—but that is probably neither feasible nor desirable. Regulating children's media use is difficult, especially in an age of internet-enabled portable devices. And there are positive effects of media. They can be educational, for instance, and they can stimulate altruistic behavior and moral development.[25] They can also be a catalyst for constructive social activities.

Even scary media, as I have suggested, can be both pleasurable and beneficial for children. Their fascination with scary material is natural, a biological mechanism through which they learn about the world and its dangers, and playing with fear can have substantial benefits—just like other kinds of play, through which children learn about the social and physical world.[26]

Of course, if you do allow or even encourage a child to engage with scary media, you should make sure that the content is appropriate. Again, I am not advocating kindergarten screenings of *The Texas Chain Saw Massacre*. But you could begin by seeking out the kind of children's horror films discussed by Catherine Lester—movies like *ParaNorman* and *Hotel Transylvania*. I would also recommend the animated movies from Japanese Studio Ghibli—*Spirited Away*, for instance, which has some quite unsettling elements, but which I think is safe (and healthy) fare for most kids over the age of eight or so. It depends on the child, of course, and if there is something particular that badly frightens a child—such as the end of the world, kidnappings, or ghosts—you should probably avoid scary movies that depict that particular threat, at least until the child has developed some tolerance for scary media.

There are several good online sources that can help you figure out whether a particular movie might be appropriate for a child, such as the British Board of Film Classification's ratings website (www.bbfc. co.uk), which has detailed descriptions of potentially frightening elements in specific movies. The website for Common Sense Media (www.commonsensemedia.org) likewise provides guidelines and age recommendations based on user-submitted reviews (including reviews from kids themselves). Finally, Into Film (www.intofilm. org) features movie reviews from children and provides information for teachers who want to use movies educationally, including scary ones.

So find appropriate material and watch it with them, for two reasons. One, watching scary stuff with kids is a lot of fun. You can tremble in suspense together, jump together, and laugh at your reactions together. You can discuss the movie during and after watching. And two, you can take the opportunity to help them develop media literacy. If there is a particularly scary scene, you can dissect it together: How does the camera move? How is lighting used to achieve a particular effect? What kind of music is there, and why? Such analysis is fun, and it helps the child learn to approach movies as construction—as artifice. If they are adept at such analysis, they are less likely to be overwhelmed by a scary movie later in life. They will know how to distance themselves from it.

Indeed, previous research has found that focusing on the unreality of a movie reduces fear responses, at least for older children.[27]

In one study, researchers recruited children from two age groups, three- to five- and nine- to 11-year-olds.[28] They were shown a three-minute scene from *The Wizard of Oz*, in which the Wicked Witch of the West has Dorothy and her little dog and is harassing a visibly distraught Dorothy. Before watching the clip, some of the children were just told that they would be watching a scene from *The Wizard of Oz*. Other children were given these unreality instructions:

> While you are watching the program, remember that it's just a story. The story is make-believe. Try to remember that Dorothy and the witch are just play-acting. Witches are pretend. The witch is just a regular person dressed in a costume. While you are watching, think of how stories like this are made to be fun to watch.[29]

After watching the clip, the children were asked how scared they had been watching the clip. Intriguingly, the older children reported significantly lower levels of fear when they had been given the unreality instructions. The younger children, in contrast, reported similar levels of fear whether they had been sensitized to the artifice of the movie or not. So a cognitive coping strategy of this kind—where one reminds oneself that it is just a movie, not real—is very effective for older children, but not for younger ones. I can relate. If somebody had told me that the corpse in the trunk of that car on the crime show was just an actor in makeup lying very still, and the fungus monster just a guy in a suit, I don't think it would have made much of a difference.

Younger children are more likely to use behavioral than cognitive coping strategies when they are scared by media. They will cover their eyes or snuggle up to somebody else or leave the room. One study recruited children from two age groups (five- to eight-year-olds and eight- to 12-year-olds) and showed them a clip from a scary movie about tarantulas overrunning a small town (*Kingdom of the Spiders*) and a suspenseful clip from a non-scary movie (*To Kill a Mockingbird*).[30] A third of the children were given no instructions, another third were told they could cover their eyes if the program became too scary, and the final third were given a remote control and told they could switch the TV off if it became too scary.

Interestingly, the young children who were told they could cover their eyes were less scared than the young children who had received different instructions. And the older children who were told they could cover their eyes were *more* scared than the older children who had been told differently. Now, the study did not measure whether actually covering one's eyes influenced fear in either direction, because very few of the kids actually covered their eyes (only eight out of the 141 who participated in the study). But it does seem that small children, who respond with fear to things that look scary, find that particular coping strategy effective.[31] Older kids can still hear the sounds and their imaginations may be unleashed, free to conjure up all manner of terrifying sights to accompany the disembodied sounds.

What if a child has already been frightened badly by some movie or television show and you weren't there to watch it with them? You could get hold of the show and watch it with them, pausing at whatever frightened them and analyzing it until the child can see the machinery producing the illusion—the zipper in the monster's back, as it were. You can also just talk to the child—take their fright reaction seriously, even if it seems ridiculous, and listen. Joanne Cantor, who is a specialist in children's fright reactions to media, has found that to be effective.[32] Also, if their traumatic encounter with scary media happened very recently, you can have the child play some Tetris. Why? I will tell you in the last chapter.

So, should you be nervous about children watching horror movies? Yes, in some cases. There is a wealth of evidence pointing to negative effects of especially premature exposure; children watching stuff they should not have been watching. At the same time, trying to shield a child from all scary stories may be a very bad idea. A gradual mastery of horror may give children crucial coping skills and function as a kind of stress inoculation. Help ease them into it. Even if you are not convinced that some horror can be good for kids, you can be sure that any child will eventually be exposed to frightening media, whether at a sleepover, unsupervised YouTube browsing, or whatever. If they have been shielded from such fare for all their lives, there is a very good chance that they will be paralyzed by the experience. Help them approach it as representation. Watch mildly scary stuff with them and help them become junior movie analysts. That way you will help them reap the benefits of horror without the negative effects.

Box 7.1 Child-Friendly Scary Movies to Watch with Young'uns

In addition to the already-mentioned child-friendly scary movies, here are some suggestions for family-friendly spooky watching (with an indication of each film's MPAA rating):

- *The Addams Family* (1991, dir. Barry Sonnenfeld), PG-13
- *Coraline* (2009, dir. Henry Selick), PG
- *Frankenweenie* (2012, dir. Tim Burton), PG
- *The Gate* (1987, dir. Tibor Takács), PG-13
- *Goosebumps* (2015, dir. Rob Letterman), PG
- *Monster House* (2006, dir. Gil Kenan), PG
- *The Nightmare before Christmas* (1993, dir. Henry Selick), PG
- *Wallace & Gromit: The Curse of the Were-Rabbit* (2005, dir. Steve Box and Nick Park), G
- *The Watcher in the Woods* (1980, dir. John Hough), PG
- *The Witches* (1990, dir. Nicolas Roeg), PG

8

"I'm Nervous about What the Popularity of Horror Says about Society"

As we have seen, more and more horror movies are made. Nowadays, hundreds of new horror movies come out each year. Should we be concerned? Is each new horror movie like a fresh and festering boil on a rapidly deteriorating patient—a symptom, in other words, of a sick society?

No, it is not quite that simple. First, it is not just horror movie production that is increasing, it is movie production *in general*. The proportion of horror movies does seem to be higher than ever before, but not radically so. About 21% of all American movies released in the 1980s have a "horror" tag, according to IMDb. For the 2010s, that number is 25%, and for the 2000s, it's 18%. The 1990s did see a slump in horror movie production—only 11% of American movies released in that decade have a "horror" tag. Anyway, as I have said before, it is not like the appetite for scary stories is new. It is ancient, part of who we are as a species. People are just finding new ways of satisfying that appetite, and with digital technologies for making and disseminating moving pictures, that medium is becoming increasingly pervasive.

Second, horror movies may serve important functions on a cultural scale, as imaginative articulations of widespread anxieties.[1] As Stephen King put it in his wonderful nonfiction book on horror, *Danse Macabre*, horror movies can "serve as an extraordinarily accurate barometer of those things which trouble the night-thoughts of a whole society."[2] Those horror movies that really resonate with people—movies like *The Exorcist* or *Night of the Living Dead* or *The*

Shining—tap into and engage with real issues, no matter how ridiculously far-fetched they may seem on the surface. An ancient demon possessing a young girl? The recently dead rising from their graves to feed on the flesh of the living? A hotel haunted by evil ghosts? Yeah, that stuff is far-fetched, but these films used those far-fetched premises to articulate troubling thoughts that were keeping America up at night.

Monsters, Literal and Metaphorical

Many horror movies—maybe the best ones—work on two levels: a literal and a metaphorical one. The same goes for the monsters that populate the genre. Take the zombie. On the literal level, it is a reanimated, decomposing corpse with severe cognitive impairment and an insatiable taste for living flesh. That is a nasty creature—dangerous, disgusting, impossible to reason with. At the same time and on a deeper level, the zombie has rich metaphorical potential. In George Romero's *Dawn of the Dead*, for example, the zombies converge on a shopping mall where they mill around mindlessly (Fig. 8.1). The symbolism is pretty obvious. Or take the vampire. It is an undead, bloodthirsty, predatory creature—but one that can symbolize pretty much everything from our deepest fears to our most burning desires. Good old Count Dracula, for example, symbolized the fear of predatory foreigners infiltrating the heart of the British Empire, whereas the glittery vampires of present-day paranormal romance personify something close to divine achievement—insanely good looks, endless wealth, superhuman strength.

Nasty monsters such as zombies and old-school vampires are mainstays of popular culture because they have a direct pipeline to our evolved fear system. You do not have to have a university degree in film study to find zombies disgusting or vampires frightening. Indeed, those monsters have traits that target primitive biological defense systems, and even nonhuman primates would find them frightening. I am not trying to be cute or flip here. Scientists have

Figure 8.1 Many horror movies work on a literal as well as a symbolic level, and the genre has a rich tradition of offering social commentary. In this shot from George A. Romero's *Dawn of the Dead* (Laural Group, 1978), the living dead are shambling toward a shopping mall. The satire is palpable.

actually investigated nonhuman primates' responses to zombies and vampires.

One team of researchers set out to investigate whether the so-called uncanny valley phenomenon is uniquely human. The uncanny valley describes our emotional response to a humanlike creature. The concept comes from a Japanese roboticist, Masahiro Mori, who back in 1970 wondered how humans would respond to increasingly humanlike robots. His intuition was that the more humanlike a robot becomes, the better we like it—the more positive our emotional response. But only up until a point when the robot becomes too humanlike for comfort and our emotional response plummets and becomes negative. When the robot is so humanlike that it is indistinguishable from an actual human being, our response goes right back up. So it is that dip in emotional valence that—when plotted on a graph with human likeness on the x-axis and emotional valence on the y-axis—looks like a valley, and which Mori called the uncanny valley (Fig. 8.2).[3] His basic idea has since been supported

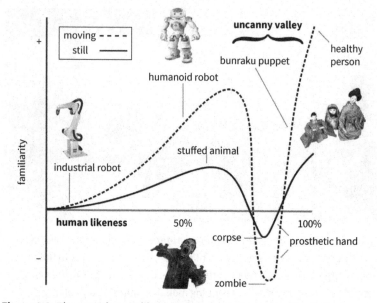

Figure 8.2 The more humanlike a creature is, the better we like it—but only up until a point. Then it becomes too humanoid for comfort, and our emotional response plummets. The response becomes positive again once a creature is very humanlike. That too-close-for-comfort dip in emotional response is called the "uncanny valley." Illustration constructed from stock images in the public domain.

by a wealth of research,[4] and it helps explain why such humanoid creatures as zombies tend to freak us out.

So the research team that wanted to see if the uncanny value was unique to the world of human affairs used Photoshop to construct zombified images of macaques.[5] They then showed those images to real macaques—cute little monkeys that live in Asia and North Africa. The result? The macaques did not like to look at those zombie cousins at all. They hollered and looked away. The zombie macaque study suggests that the uncanny valley is not, in fact, unique to us humans, but that it has its roots in ancient primate psychology—presumably as a disease-avoidance mechanism. We evolved to be cautious around individuals who diverge significantly from the species norm, simply because of the risk that they carry an infectious disease that has made them look "off."[6] Macaques do the same thing.

In another study, a research team got it into their heads to try to scare zoo animals with Halloween masks. (You gotta love science!) They had already scared college students with the masks, but they wanted to see whether something more fundamental than cultural conditioning was at play. Maybe the college students had just learned to associate a werewolf mask with horror films and thus with goosebumps and trepidation, say. The researchers figured they could test this by seeing whether nonhuman animals would be afraid of those masks. So the researchers tried to feed a bunch of different zoo animals—including a chimp, a baboon, a couple of lions, a wild boar, some macaws, and a camel—while wearing different masks.[7] If the animals responded fearfully to the masks, then something more fundamental than culture must be responsible.

The researchers had a selection of 13 masks. Those masks ranged from not scary at all to very scary, according to the college students. For example, a Bill Clinton mask was not seen as scary. A *Scream* mask—a distorted face—was seen as pretty scary. Scariest of all was a grotesque, grayish, furious-looking vampire mask with a wide-open mouth full of fangs. A researcher would wear a mask and offer the animals some food, and another researcher would time how long it took the animals to accept the food. The longer the so-called latency, the researchers figured, the more freaked out the animal.

So what happened? Well, the primates, especially, were unnerved by the masks. Take Joe the chimp. When a researcher offered him food without a mask on, Joe took it after six seconds. With the Bill Clinton mask on, seven seconds. But with the vampire mask, a whole 15 seconds passed before Joe took the bait. And Joe was actually pretty fearless, compared to the other primates. On average, for the primate group, seven seconds elapsed before they took the food when the researcher wasn't wearing a mask—compared to a full 81 seconds when he was wearing the vampire mask. The results for the non-primates were more mixed. Take Jimmy the Bactrian camel. He did not care much whether the researcher was wearing a mask or not.

It took him three seconds to take the food from the non-masked researcher, but still only five seconds when the researcher was wearing a Michael Myers mask. (Myers is the chillingly cold-blooded killer of *Halloween*.)

These cool studies suggest that nonhuman primates would find zombie and vampire movies frightening. It is not that the macaques would look at the zombie macaque and think, "Oh my God, what a terrifying vision of mindless consumerism!" And Spencer the spider monkey didn't wait a full two minutes to take food from the researcher in the vampire mask because he was horrified by the ambivalent vision of eternal but parasitic life encoded into the vampire visage. No, those primates responded to very literal cues of threat—cues of contagion and predation.

For us humans, the situation is more complicated. Like the monkeys and apes, we respond to those literal cues of contagion and predation. The cues fast-track their way through the brain.[8] In addition, though, we may respond to the symbolic significance of monsters and the imaginative worlds they inhabit. Maybe the most long-lived horror movies are those that manage simultaneously to shock the inner primate and haunt the human heart.

Horror Movies and Cultural Context

Let us return to *The Exorcist*. Now, that film did a great job of freaking people out, as we have seen—audiences were grossed out by the graphic depictions of body fluids and violations, and they were deeply unnerved at the realistic-looking representation of an evil demon taking control of an innocent young girl, with murder and mayhem to follow. But it also struck a deeper nerve—it managed to attach some mightily powerful images to those night-thoughts that Stephen King talked about.

When *The Exorcist* came out in 1973, many Americans felt that they were living in weird and tumultuous times. The Vietnam War was raging, cultural and generational fault lines were opening up, and traditional institutions seemed to be toppling. Young people were demonstrating against the war and corrupt politicians. At Kent State, in 1970, a student peace rally turned bloody when National Guardsmen opened fire on unarmed protesters, killing four and wounding nine. Against this riotous cultural backdrop appeared *The Exorcist*, in which "audiences witnessed the graphic desecration of everything that was considered wholesome and good about the fading American dream—the home, the family, the church and, most shockingly, the child,"[9] as the film critic Mark Kermode puts it.

In *The Exorcist*, everything goes to hell because an ancient evil finds a host in sweet Regan. Happily, all that is needed to put things right again are a couple of good men, Father Karras and Father Merrin, who together manage to exorcise the demon. Why Regan, though? The film does not say so explicitly, but it suggests that she is vulnerable to this force of evil because she is growing up in a broken family—her parents are getting a divorce—and being raised by a godless single mother. That is not good, at least from the conservative, Catholic perspective of William Peter Blatty, who produced the film and wrote the screenplay. As Kermode says, "Here on screen was a clear-cut struggle between good and evil in which priests, policemen, good mothers and devoted sons fought a righteous battle to release rebellious, parent-hating children from the grip of a lustful, all-consuming devil."[10] You see the symbolic connection between Regan turning into a foul-mouthed, mother-hating family-wrecker and then those unwashed hippies trying to stick it to The Man and overturn The System.

So *The Exorcist* is very much a child of its times, one that reflected widespread tensions and anxieties in its depiction of an all-American girl suddenly infected with an obscene, out-of-control evil. The thematic resonance between the film and its cultural context likely contributed to its powerful effect, even as the people watching it may not have consciously made that connection. Even so, they may have registered, if even subconsciously, that here was a film that was about more than a literal demon possessing a girl—a film that somehow articulated something that had been nagging at them, something to do with the cultural, moral, and political tensions that surrounded them.

Consider another example of horror movies as diagnostic of cultural context—the 1955 horror and sci-fi story *The Body Snatchers* by Jack Finney. That story has been adapted for the big screen several times, most famously with the 1956 film *Invasion of the Body Snatchers* and with the 1978 version of the same title. The plot is fairly simple. Seeds from outer space land in a small city in California. The seeds grow into humanlike pod people—replicas of the original inhabitants, who disappear as they are replaced by the pod people. The pod people look just like them and have all their memories and mannerisms, only they have no emotions, no real individuality. That storyline seems to have been nourished by Cold War paranoia and stoked by a general fear of conformity as well as a more specific fear that your neighbor might be an evil commie, a secret red agent pretending to be a solid American.

Another Cold War horror movie, John Carpenter's *The Thing* from 1982, likewise tapped into the paranoia of its time. That movie is also about an alien life form, a parasite that assimilates and then imitates other organisms. It infiltrates a research base in Antarctica, taking the shape first of a dog and then of various members of the research team. In one famously tense scene, the main character, MacReady, is trying to figure out who of his comrades has been assimilated by the alien life form (and so has alien blood running through his veins). He devises a test to reveal the impostor, figuring that he can draw it out by putting a red-hot copper wire to some of its blood on the assumption that every piece of the Thing is "an individual animal with a built-in desire to protect its own life." As he says: "When a man bleeds, it's just tissue. But blood from one of you Things won't obey when it's attacked. It'll try and survive. Crawl away from a hot needle, say."

MacReady ties up his comrades and procures some blood from each one. Tension mounts as he touches the copper wire to each blood sample in turn. There is no background music, just the nerve-flaying sound of the arctic wind blowing incessantly outside the isolated research station. The camera glides from anxious face to anxious face, dwells on the blood sample, zooms in on the idle flamethrower that MacReady uses to heat his copper wire, goes back to the anxious faces. Each time MacReady touches the copper wire to a blood sample, there is a bit of smoke and a loud sizzle (Fig. 8.3). Phew, human. Not an alien impostor . . . until, finally, hot copper meets alien blood and the blood jumps out of the petri dish with a startling screech. The impostor has been identified. The scene, and the movie as a whole, is a slow-burn paranoia fest that powerfully exploits a basic human predicament—Who can you trust? Can you ever really know what is inside other people's minds?—and resonates in particular with a cultural climate of mistrust and fear.

Of course, some horror movies are more obviously and more directly plugged into a zeitgeist—the spirit of the time—than others. The ones that do manage to tap into contemporary concerns may hit contemporary audiences particularly hard; they may also become dated more quickly than those horror movies that are more keenly attuned to universal predicaments, such as *Jaws*, which is about a fairly uncultured fear of being eaten by a huge predator. And some

Figure 8.3 Horror movies reflect their cultural context. John Carpenter's slow-burn horror/sci-fi movie *The Thing* (Turman-Foster, 1982), about a parasitical alien entity infiltrating a research station in Antarctica, provides a vivid reflection of Cold War paranoia. Here MacReady (Kurt Russell) attempts to determine via a blood test which of his camp members have been parasitized.

horror movie directors may deliberately set out to articulate those night-thoughts to which King referred.

Take Jordan Peele's 2017 hit movie *Get Out*, which is about a group of white people abducting African Americans whom they auction off to old, rich white people who are looking for young, healthy bodies. The buyer's brain is then transplanted into the slave's body. Peele said that he wanted to criticize the idea of a post-racial America— a post-Obama America free of racism—by depicting "limousine liberals" and their subtle racism, and the ongoing oppression of African Americans.[11] In *Get Out*, the African American victims are colonized by the whites in a very literal way. Now, the plot element of having your body taken over by another consciousness, with the complete loss of agency such a thing entails, is just fundamentally frightening. All possession horror films play on that fear.[12] But Peele appropriated that horror trope and used it in a politically progressive movie, a horror film with an overt ideological agenda.

Given horror's ability to articulate night-thoughts and probe what King called "phobic pressure points," are some cultural eras more hospitable to horror than others? I have suggested that the Cold War era, with its free-floating paranoia, may have been a hotbed for at least a particular kind of horror movie, one that feeds off such paranoia and offers vivid scenarios of deceptive evil. While I do not think there are any eras or cultures without horror—since the thirst for frightening fiction is deeply embedded in human nature—it could well be that some eras, and some cultures, are more hospitable to horror than others. Certainly, many critics have suggested that periods of great sociocultural turmoil are particularly conducive to the genre, which seems like a reasonable assumption to me. People living through such times may feel a stronger need to confront fear through the threat simulations offered by horror.

Some critics have taken that assumption and given it an extra twist, suggesting that the American horror movie thrives particularly well in conservative times—for instance, whenever there is a Republican behind the desk in the Oval Office. I am not sure why that should be the case—maybe those critics think that horror works best when it challenges the status quo as enforced by a conservative administration, or that life under conservative rule is horrible and thus conducive to stories that encode the horror of existence—but I have heard the idea bandied around at conferences for horror scholars, and the researcher Murray Leeder says in his book *Horror Film: A Critical Introduction* that "conservative periods" provide "fertile ground for horror filmmakers."[13] Is that really the case?

We can get a preliminary fix on the claim by looking at horror movie production over time compared with the political orientation of the administration. That is what I did in the graph in Figure 8.4. I harvested American feature-length horror-tagged movies with at least 50 votes from the period 1961 (the beginning of John F. Kennedy's presidency) to 2019 from the Internet Movie Database. I chose this timeframe because it gives me four eras of Democratic administration and four with Republican administration.

On the face of it, it does look like there is a surge in horror movie production whenever there is a Republican administration, with a spike in the early 1970s (when Nixon was in office) and again in the

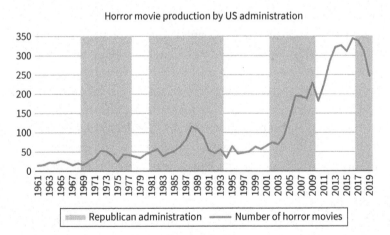

Horror movie production by US administration

Figure 8.4 Do conservative eras provide especially fertile soil for horror movie production, as some scholars have claimed? No, it does not seem to be quite that simple. This graph shows the number of American horror movies made in the period 1961–2019; eras with Republican administration are shaded gray. Data harvested from the Internet Movie Database.

late 1980s (when Reagan was in office), and then another huge spike in the early 2000s (when Bush Jr. was in office). However, there is also a huge spike during Obama's presidency, and a marked drop during Trump's presidency.

So we are not looking at a simple correlation here, and we should also keep in mind that there is usually a delay of several years from the moment somebody gets an idea for a horror movie to the opening of the movie in theaters. A film released when there is a conservative administration may have been conceived and made under a liberal administration, and vice versa. And of course, my graph only gets at quantity, not quality. It could be that the horror movies produced in conservative eras are particularly good, but that does not seem to be the case, at least if we take IMDb ratings as indicators of quality. The average IMDb rating of horror movies went down over the 12-year period of the Reagan-Bush administration.[14]

Let us dwell, for a moment, on that salient spike in horror movies in the late 1980s. It is probably driven at least partly by slasher movies, which were huge in that decade, with several influential franchises—*Halloween*, *Friday the 13th*, and *Nightmare on Elm Street*—and hundreds of knock-offs. Cultural critics have interpreted the slasher film as a conservative backlash to progressive movements, as I mentioned previously, with liberated youthful characters being punished by a masked enforcer of the status quo.[15] That interpretation has shaped the genre itself, such that the postmodern slasher film *Scream* from 1996 had a character list the rules for surviving a horror film: "There are certain *rules* that one must abide by in order to successfully survive a horror movie. For instance, number one: you can never have sex. Big no-no! Big no-no! Sex equals death, okay? Number two: You can never drink or do drugs. The sin factor. It's a sin! It's an extension of number one."

Empirical research has suggested that it is not quite that simple. A team of researchers analyzed the 30 top-grossing slasher films from three decades (1980 to 2010) and found that, yes, characters who are shown nude have very high mortality in slasher films—but it is not the case that only virgins survive, and it is also not the case that ethnic minority characters inevitably get slashed.[16] Still, 1980s slasher movies have been widely regarded as reflecting the conservative values of the Reagan administration.

However, it is not just horror movie production that increases during the Reagan-Bush administration. In the graph shown in Figure 8.5, I plotted the number of horror movies made in this period and, for comparison, the number of comedies as well as the total number of feature films from this era.

If those middle to late 1980s were particularly hospitable to horror, they were also particularly hospitable to comedy—indeed, to movies in general. Movie production increased dramatically at this time, with the rapid growth in independent filmmaking and the game-changing emergence of the home video market. Horror movies, like any kind of movie, are subject to all kinds of influences. I am not convinced that conservative eras are especially conducive to horror movies; the data does not seem to support the idea.

Yes, horror movies reflect their context, and yes, some horror movie creators use political dissatisfaction as fuel for their frightening art. Jordan Peele is just one example; many of the young

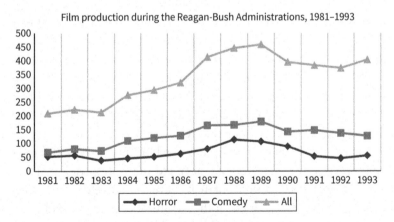

Figure 8.5 A closer look at US movie production under the Reagan-Bush administrations. The graph shows the total number of films made, as well as the number of horror movies and comedy movies for comparison. It's not just horror movies that spike in the late-1980s. Data harvested from the Internet Movie Database.

directors of the innovative and often bleak horror films of the 1970s—George Romero, Tobe Hooper, and Wes Craven, to name a few—used their art at least partly as an outlet for their political frustration.[17] As the horror sociologist Todd Platts has noted, something interesting happened to American horror movies by the late 1960s. Up until then, most horror movies were relatively innocent and ultimately upbeat, vanquishing evil in the end and leaving their audiences with a sense of hope. But by 1968, with the emergence of the New Horror, the genre "began taking a dark and twisted turn by directly commenting, increasingly critically, on contemporary American life and institutions and locating the monstrous within us rather than away from us."[18] Of course we can identify earlier films that fit this description—such as Hitchcock's *Psycho*, which also subverted audience expectations and portrayed a monster from within—but something peculiar does seem to be happening with horror movies toward the end of the decade.

A good example is Romero's landmark 1968 movie *Night of the Living Dead*, which used the zombie apocalypse to depict the collapse of a tiny society—a group of people barricaded against the living dead in a farmhouse in the American heartland. They fail to cooperate and keep quarrelling, eventually killing each other or getting each other killed. The film depicted human nature at its worst, and it did so against a bloody background: the disastrous Tet Offensive in Vietnam, for example, and the shocking political assassinations of Martin Luther King and Robert F. Kennedy. We are our own worst enemy, the film seemed to suggest, and news stories of the day would have appeared to corroborate the idea.

So horror movies are always enmeshed in, and a product of, their cultural context. They are good at mirroring widespread anxieties and concerns, as I have said, but there is a more concrete way in which horror movies are products of their cultural context. Consider, for instance, how the motion picture technology available to filmmakers at a given time has a decisive influence on their art. Take the invention of sound in the cinema. Nowadays, a silent horror movie is almost inconceivable; we have seen how important sound is to the jump scare, for example. Similarly, widescreen cinematography gave horror directors a new tool for frightening the audience, essentially giving them a much wider canvas on which to paint their fearsome pictures (Fig. 8.6).[19] And the explosive growth in slasher movies in the 1980s was driven, at least in part, by developments in prosthetics technology and visual effects in general.[20] Special effects people got much better at creating gory spectacles on screen. More recently, computer-generated imagery has made it possible for filmmakers to create incredibly realistic monsters (and mutilations) on screen.

Then there is the structure of the movie business itself, which determines what movies get made, what kind of distribution they get, how much creative control is left in the hands of the director, and so on. I mentioned in a previous chapter the surge of well-produced horror movies in the new millennium—what some critics contentiously referred to as "elevated horror." Well, that surge is not solely due to some zeitgeist, some cultural current of anxiety post-9/11, say, but has to be seen also against the backdrop of structural conditions in the movie business. At a time when budgets for Hollywood movies routinely exceed $100 million and producers seem to be drawn mainly to superhero flicks, independent horror-happy production

Figure 8.6 In *Halloween* (Compass International Pictures/Falcon International Pictures, 1978), director John Carpenter and his cinematographer Dean Cundey masterfully used the anamorphic widescreen format to unsettle their viewers, for example by using unbalanced compositions with large areas of darkness out of which anything might emerge.

companies with a simple recipe—tiny budgets and creative control to directors—have found a lucrative niche.

The emergence of the stunningly successful Blumhouse Productions, for instance, has been a watershed event in the history of the American horror film. Blumhouse has given us *Get Out*, the *Insidious* movies, the *Sinister* movies—and of course the *Paranormal Activity* franchise. The first movie in that franchise, *Paranormal Activity*, was made for a measly $15,000. Its global box office is $193 million. That's a serious return on investment. The film, which is about a young couple whose tract home appears to be haunted by a demon, is shot in a documentary style and was made with a tiny crew. The people behind the film thus managed to turn budgetary constraints into an advantage—it is the claustrophobic atmosphere of the setting, which is almost completely confined to the couple's home, and the crude authenticity of the cinematography that give this movie its raw power. The film really looks like a home movie, and that is what makes it so terrifying. Some critics have further suggested that the film resonated with a widespread sense of financial and personal insecurity in the wake of 9/11 and the economic recession of 2008.[21] *Paranormal Activity*, in other words, managed to take advantage of salient anxieties—both topical concerns over safety and security and more deep-seated fears of assault from unknown forces—and the availability of cheap recording equipment and existing distribution channels to reach a huge audience and become a major hit. Cultural context matters.

Horror Movies as Symptom and Cure

Horror movies are effective when they resonate with us, and they can do so by depicting material that would frighten the fur off our primate cousins and by depicting material that in more or less subtle ways articulates cultural anxieties. There is, unfortunately, no empirical science on horror movies' culture-scale therapeutic effects—I do not know whether a society with many horror movies is more healthy than a society with few horror movies—but I do not think that the profusion of horror movies is a symptom of a sick society. A troubled society, maybe, but horror movies may be both symptom and at least part of the cure. People use horror movies not just for fearful pleasure and socializing, but for making sense of the world around them.

When the coronavirus pandemic swept across the globe in 2020, fiction movies about pandemics surged to the top of streaming lists. A few months into the pandemic, Steven Soderbergh's 2011 film *Contagion*, about a pandemic outbreak of a new respiratory virus not unlike the coronavirus, rapidly rose from being the 270th most-watched Warner Bros. film to become the second most-watched film from that company.[22] The 1995 film *Outbreak*, a grisly depiction of an Ebola outbreak, got second wind on Netflix. It seems a little weird. In the spring and early summer months of 2020, nations all over the world were going into lockdown overnight. Stores and hospitals were quickly running out of protective equipment. A lot of people were dying from COVID-19, and the news carried horrifying stories of mass graves being dug to compensate for overflowing morgues. So why, against this backdrop of death and contagious doom, were lots of people seeking out pandemic fiction? Did they not have enough of contagion and disease around them?

Probably yes, but at the same time, people were trying to make sense of a situation that to them was unprecedented. Presumably, they were unconsciously trying to cope by consulting fiction that depicted similar situations, like a lost wanderer consulting a map. Fiction has for centuries depicted the end of the world. The Bible has a pretty spectacular doomsday scenario, and literature brims with end-of-the-world depictions, such as the apocalyptic pandemics described in George R. Stewart's *Earth Abides* from 1949 and John Christopher's *Empty World* from 1977. Likewise, the world has been destroyed a thousand times on the silver screen, both in realistic and in more fanciful versions such as zombie apocalypse movies.

Even a far-fetched zombie movie can tell us something about social and psychological dynamics during large-scale crises. When the Centers for Disease Control and Prevention in 2011 launched their zombie preparedness campaign—"If you're ready for a zombie apocalypse, then you're ready for any emergency"—they were only half kidding. What does it take to survive a zombie apocalypse? Canned goods, bottled water, first-aid materials, escape plans, battery-operated means of communication, people on whom you can depend. And guns, of course. Lots of guns. What does it take to survive a natural disaster? Pretty much the same things, except hopefully you can do without the guns. I don't think people watch those movies to learn about what goes into a prepper kit, but I do think there is a learning potential there. Those movies can teach us about the qualities of experience under situations of great upheaval; they can teach us what it feels like to suddenly find that the ground you have been standing on is crumbling.[23]

Horror movies can help us confront our fears and put concrete images to abstract anxieties, and maybe, by confronting our anxiety in the context of make-believe, we get better at handling it. In the midst of the coronavirus pandemic, I teamed up with a group of researchers to see whether people who had watched a lot of horror and apocalyptic movies were doing a better job of coping with the pandemic.[24] As it turns out, horror fans did report better resilience—less psychological distress—in the midst of the pandemic, suggesting that the many hours they had spent watching scary movies had helped them refine their emotion regulation skills. Horror fans, we think, become better at managing their own fear—at keeping negative emotions at a tolerable level, presumably because they have much experience with emotion regulation during horror movie watching. They simply have more practice coping with fear and anxiety than people who steer clear of scary movies. We also found that people who watch a lot of what we call "prepper movies"—movies about alien invasions, zombies, and the apocalypse—reported less psychological distress *and* better preparedness. They were not as blindsided by the pandemic and the upheavals it caused as people who do not watch those kinds of films because they had imaginatively simulated similar scenarios many times before.

So horror movies are symptomatic of a culture's fears. A culture of fear is likely to nourish the horror genre, but then, I don't know that there has ever been a culture on this fine planet that was not a culture of fear. At least, it looks like we can use horror movies to articulate and actively confront the fears that haunt our culture.

9

"Okay, I'm Ready to Watch a Horror Movie. What Now?"

Hopefully, by now, you will be less nervous about horror movies. Now, it was never my mission to eradicate that nervousness completely—there *are* good reasons to be nervous about horror. People do have bad experiences with horror, as I have mentioned, and horror is meant to sting. If you do not feel the slightest apprehension as you are about to watch a new horror movie, either you are a rare exception or the horror movie industry is in big trouble. But if you are now convinced that the benefits of horror can outweigh the costs and are about ready to watch a horror movie, let me give you some final advice on how to keep your fear response at a tolerable level. Most of it is pretty commonsensical, but there is science to support it.

Don't Watch a Horror Movie Alone

Most people are more frightened by horror movies when they watch them alone than when they watch them with others.[1] It is not really surprising. *Homo sapiens* is a highly social animal, and we feel more vigilant and anxious when we are alone than when we are around others.[2] It makes biological sense. We have always been more vulnerable to attack on our own. Even though a horror movie poses no real threat—it is a threat simulation—the principle applies. Personally, I would never watch a horror movie alone. Whenever I have to travel for work, I always make sure to bring some non-horrific reading material for the journey, and usually opt for a sci-fi or action movie when I am alone in the hotel room at night.

There are two caveats to my advice against watching horror movies alone, though. The first caveat is that fear can be modified in either direction by social influences. The presence of calm others can dampen your fear . . . and the presence of terrified others can enhance your fear. Fear, like other emotions, can be contagious.[3] We evolved to mirror other people's emotional state. If you are surrounded by people who are terrified, you are bound to catch some of that sentiment, even if you do not register any threat. A German study found that if research subjects watch clips from scary films in the company of people who scream at frightening scenes, they will report higher levels of fear in response to the clip than if their co-watchers do not scream.[4] So you should select your co-viewers carefully. You might not want to assemble a whole crew of scaredy-cats, but on the other hand, it is no fun to watch a serious horror movie with people who do not take it seriously.

The second caveat is that shared activities are experienced as being more intense. In one study, participants were given some delicious chocolate to eat in the company of another person.[5] When both individuals ate chocolate, participants would say the chocolate tasted better than if the other person was doing something else, like reading an art book. Simply sharing the experience made participants find the stimulus, the chocolate, more pleasurable. In a follow-up study, participants were given some very dark and unpleasant-tasting chocolate. Intriguingly, when both individuals ate bitter chocolate at the same time, participants would rate the chocolate more unpleasant than if the other person was absorbed in another task. So it is not that sharing an experience makes it more pleasurable, necessarily; sharing an experience amplifies it.

Watching a horror film with others is thus likely to amplify the experience, if we can generalize from the chocolate study, and I think that we probably can. That may mean more intense fear, which is probably counteracted by the feeling of safety that comes from being in the presence of others, as well as more intense pleasure. Watching movies together is more fun than watching them alone.

Don't Watch Horror Movies in a Movie Theater

As I have mentioned before, modern multiplex movie theaters are designed for maximum immersion and minimal distraction.[6] Once the lights go down, your attention will be inexorably directed toward the screen in front of you, and that screen is designed to fill out your visual field—to really colonize your visual perception. A state-of-the-art sound system makes sure that your auditory world is dominated by the movie's soundtrack. Walls are painted black to be inconspicuous, and seats are incredibly comfortable so that it almost feels as if you are floating in the air. Maximum immersion, minimal distraction. The thing is, the more immersed you are—absorbed in the fictional events, feeling like you are in the fictional world—the stronger your emotional responses are likely to be.[7]

Sound is absolutely crucial to the horror movie.[8] To provide a highly immersive soundscape, state-of-the-art cinema sound systems use an eight-channel surround configuration (Dolby Surround 7.1). That is three channels in front of you (left, center, and right), one on each side, and two in the back, as well as a subwoofer (the so-called LFE or low frequency effects channel). You will be enveloped in sound, and sound is extremely effective in inducing emotion. It can even subtly influence your perception.

An intriguing study showed research participants ambiguous pictures—drawings that can be interpreted in two ways, just like the classic optical illusion that looks like an old lady or a young woman with a feather in her hair (you can look it up online; it is sometimes called "My Wife and My Mother-in-Law"). In this study, each of the three pictures could be interpreted either as a neutral or as a threatening image. One showed a squirrel or an alligator, depending on perspective; another showed a coiled rope or a coiled snake, and the final picture showed either a pot or a cleaver. Now, the pictures were accompanied either by no music, by happy instrumental music (Grieg's "Morning Mood"), or by scary instrumental music (Penderecki's "Threnody to the Victims of Hiroshima").

When participants listened to no music or to happy music, they tended to perceive the neutral versions of the images—squirrel, rope, and pot. But when they listened to fearful music, they were far more likely to arrive at a threatening interpretation—they would see an alligator, a snake, and a cleaver (Fig. 9.1).[9] As the study shows, sound can influence perception via emotional stimulation. The scary music

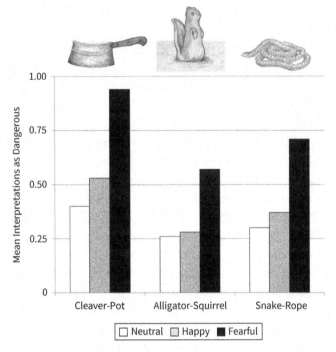

Figure 9.1 Scary music biases visual perception. If you look at an ambiguous image while listening to scary music, you're likely to see danger in the image—a cleaver rather than a pot, an alligator rather than a squirrel, or a snake rather than a coil of rope. The graph shows how participants in Prinz and Seidel's study interpreted such ambiguous images. Participants saw images while listening to no music, happy music, or fearful music. If they provided a benign interpretation, their response was coded as 0. If they provided a dangerous interpretation, their response was coded as 1. The graph shows how participants, on average, interpreted the images. The closer to 0, the more people gave a benign interpretation; the closer to 1, the more people gave a dangerous interpretation.

From "Alligator or Squirrel: Musically Induced Fear Reveals Threat in Ambiguous Figures" (https://journals.sagepub.com/doi/abs/10.1068/p7290). Reproduced with generous permission.

likely sensitized the participants' fear systems and primed their vigilance, prompting them to perceive threat in those ambiguous images. Presumably, something similar happens in horror movies. That creepy background music is not just ornamentation; it helps to get you in the right mood and has you anxiously scanning the screen for danger, interpreting ambiguous or even innocuous cues as threats.

Certain sound configurations reliably set your nervous system on edge. I mentioned previously the importance of sound to the cinematic jump-scare—without those acoustic blasts or stingers, the jump scares would lose much of their power to startle. Similarly, sound artists will often mix inherently disturbing sounds into horror movie soundtracks, such as the animal distress sounds mimicked by the screeching violins in *Psycho*'s shower scene or the slaughterhouse noises mixed into the soundtrack of *The Exorcist*.[10] Similarly, so-called drones are very often used to create tension and instill a sense of dread.[11] The drone, which is a sustained note or chord—a droning sound that just goes on and on—was used as early as the 1931 horror movie *Dr. Jekyll and Mr. Hyde* and occurs very often in horror movies today. The terrifying *Hereditary*, for example, uses drones quite heavily and to great effect. There is something deeply disturbing about an unwavering, unresolved sound without an obvious source. Indeed, the movie music expert Neil Lerner speculates that the raw, atavistic power of sound in horror movies can be connected to our species' deep past as prey animals constantly scanning our auditory environments for cues of danger—the sudden pounding of a predator's footfalls, say, or the bone-stirring rumbling of an approaching thunderstorm or earthquake.[12]

It is pretty easy to obstruct a visual signal—you cover or close your eyes. But you cannot very effectively obstruct an auditory signal, partly because we do not just listen with our ears. Sound is vibration, and a powerful low-frequency sound can get one's body vibrating, causing intense discomfort or even dread. Deaf people can register powerful sounds through chest vibrations. Some horror directors have allegedly experimented with sounds at such low frequencies that they are felt more than heard—and the LFE channel in surround systems is perfect for the job.[13] The director of the French extreme horror movie *Irréversible*, Gaspar Noe, allegedly used barely perceptible low-frequency sound to unsettle his audience. When the movie was screened at the Cannes Film Festival in 2002, hundreds of people walked out and 20 audience members fainted during the film. Noe said that he had added sound at 27 Hz—barely perceptible to the human ear—to the first half hour of the film, with the intention of unnerving his audience.[14] I guess it worked, although people may have had other reasons to walk out, of course.

I mentioned previously the BBC mockumentary *Ghostwatch*, which terrified a lot of viewers because they were duped by the authentic look and the use of actual, well-known, and trusted television personalities. Stephen Volk, who wrote the script, had a great idea: he wanted to add ultrasound to the soundtrack—sounds at such high frequencies that they would be outside the human hearing range. His idea was that such sounds would agitate the viewers' dogs and cats. Imagine that. You are watching what appears to be a documentary about an actual case of paranormal activity, on distinguished BBC1 no less, and other viewers are phoning in with their stories about ghosts. (The phone-ins were staged, of course.) And then suddenly, your own dog starts barking frantically, at nothing you can see. The cat goes nuts, trying to get out. That would have made a great gimmick, and Volk actually convinced the director to look into it, but it turned out to be technically impossible.[15]

If your goal is to keep fear at a tolerable level, you are probably better off watching a horror movie on your living room television set than in a movie theater. Even if you have a top-of-the-line home cinema sound system, you will have power over the volume. You can turn it down if you become too scared. Control—even the perception of control—is important. An old study found that if you show people nasty pictures of corpses but tell them that they can switch off the images at any time, their galvanic skin response—a measure of arousal, such as is produced by fear—is lower than if they are not given such an option.[16] This brings me to another piece of advice: do not be peer-pressured into watching a horror film against your will. The decision should be your own. In our haunted house research, we have consistently found that visitors who were internally motivated had a better time than those visitors who had been convinced by others to tag along.[17]

A few more pieces of advice before I give you some tips on how to manage your own fear once you are sitting in front of the scary movie. Do not watch horror movies at nighttime. Research has shown that we are more jumpy at night,[18] which may be a relic from a deep past when our ancestors had to be vigilant as soon as darkness fell, because that is when many hominin-hungry predators hunted . . . and they had much better night vision than our ancestors did. In prehistoric times, darkness meant danger, and it still does to our inner caveperson. And as mentioned earlier, do not watch a horror movie if you are really tired. Neuroscience studies have shown that sleep deprivation leads to quite drastically amplified amygdala activity. (The amygdala is a structure in your brain that seems to perform several tasks, but one of its main jobs is to govern the fear response.) In addition, sleep-deprived individuals seem to have poorer top-down control of amygdala activity, that is, a harder time suppressing fear.[19] Finally, get some exercise. It is good for you across the board, and research suggests a negative correlation between physical strength and fearfulness. The stronger you are, the less fearful you are—probably because you feel less vulnerable to attack.[20]

Coping Strategies and Psychological Distance

You can actively use coping strategies to keep fear down. One such strategy is the creation of psychological distance, which neuroscience has shown is effective for emotional regulation.[21] Psychological distance is a concept that indicates how close something feels to oneself, and it has four dimensions: temporal, spatial, social, and hypothetical.[22] Something that happened two years ago is more psychologically distant to you than something that happened yesterday. Similarly with something that happens in another country, to somebody else. You are likely to respond more strongly to something that is close to you—a car accident that involved your nephew yesterday, say, compared to a car accident two decades ago involving a stranger in another country. Then there is hypothetical distance, which indicates how plausible you perceive something to be. If you do not believe in ghosts, that concept is distant from you.

Now, fiction is by definition psychologically distanced because it is make-believe. The characters are made up, and so are the events. We know that whatever happens on the screen or on the page is not actually happening. Besides, fiction is about others, and it takes place elsewhere. At the same time, fiction is typically designed to create an illusion of closeness—of verisimilitude, if you want to be fancy about it. It is designed to immerse you in a fictional world and to make you care about the characters. But some stories are going to feel more psychologically close to you than other stories. In old movies, for instance, people speak a little funny and dress a little funny—which increases psychological distance. Conversely, in some stories you can really relate to the characters, partly because they are well depicted, but also maybe because they resemble you. Maybe they are struggling with similar problems, maybe they have similar personalities. In horror movies, specifically, directors will often attempt to decrease psychological distance in an attempt to increase emotional impact. Just consider all those horror movies that purport to be based on real events, or that are made to look documentary—*Ghostwatch*, for instance, or *Blair Witch Project*.

Keeping in mind the power of psychological distance may help you find horror movies that have a just-right impact. You might begin by watching old horror movies, for example—Carpenter's *Halloween* (1978), say, in which the characters wear bell-bottom jeans, or his *Christine* (1983), in which the teenage characters use quaint slang like "shitters" ("No shitter ever came between Christine and me," says the owner of the eponymous possessed car). Conversely, you should probably avoid horror movies about things that really scare you in real life, as I have already suggested. If you are concerned about home invasions, do not watch films that depict home invasions. If you believe in the supernatural, avoid supernatural horror movies and go for something psychological instead. That is a way of increasing hypothetical psychological distance. It is hardly surprising, but researchers have shown empirically that if you are afraid of a particular thing, a horror movie about such a thing is going to frighten you more.[23]

You can also manipulate psychological distance when you are watching a movie. One strategy for fear-suppression is to actively work against immersion—to avoid being sucked into the story and thus increase psychological distance. It is effective because immersion is correlated with emotional intensity.[24] It is a trade-off, though, because researchers have also found a correlation between immersion and enjoyment.[25] The more immersed you are in a fictional story, the more enjoyable the experience, apparently. But recall that haunted house study I mentioned earlier—the one in which we asked some participants to maximize their fear and other participants to minimize their fear.[26] A very common strategy among our fear minimizers was to avoid immersion and construct a so-called protective frame for themselves, for instance by reminding themselves that it was all make-believe. The point is that while the two groups reported different fear levels, they reported similar levels of enjoyment. It could be that for some people, the white-knucklers, the best horror experience comes through a distanced kind of engagement.

There is actually some empirical research to support such an idea. A study found that horror fans—defined as those people who watch horror movies at least once a month—experience co-activation of positive and negative emotions when they watch clips from horror movies.[27] They feel fear as well as enjoyment. In contrast, people who tend to avoid horror movies experience only fear when they watch clips from horror movies. For them, there is a negative correlation between fear and happiness-related emotions when they watch horror. In a fascinating follow-up study, the researchers placed their horror-reluctant participants in a protective frame—they provided some psychological distance by prompting participants to keep in mind that what they were seeing was fiction, not real. They did so by showing biographies of the actors involved in the horror movies (*The Exorcist* and *'Salem's Lot*) before actually showing the clips. They also inserted pictures of the actors along with the actors' real names alongside the clips themselves, so that participants would be continually reminded of the artifice of the clips.

Lo and behold, in the protective frame condition, the people who did not like horror reported feeling both fear and happiness-related emotions. They experienced the co-activation of negative and positive emotions that horror fans reported. So, if you are not a horror fan, adopting a protective frame is likely to reduce your fear *and* increase your pleasure.

Research from the field of empirical aesthetics supports the idea. In one study, researchers showed photographs that were either positive (such as a happy kid) or negative (such as a mutilated corpse) to participants.[28] Participants were told either that the photographs were artworks or press photographs—that is, constructed or real. They were then asked to evaluate the photos, and their emotional states were recorded. When participants looked at nasty images, they responded with similar levels of negative emotions whether they were told that the images were constructed or real. But participants claimed to like the nasty pictures better when they thought those pictures were artworks rather than documentary photos. They still felt that the images were nasty, but those nasty feelings were accompanied by aesthetic appreciation. So context matters, and how we think about a stimulus shapes our emotional response to it. Reminding yourself that a horror movie is just a movie might increase your liking of it (and keep you from fainting, as the marketing campaign for the rape-revenge movie *Last House on the Left* admonished, Fig. 9.2).

A psychologically distanced form of engaging with horror movies not only serves to keep fear at a tolerable level, but may also open a whole other can of pleasure for the novice horror viewer: aesthetic pleasure. If you view the horror movie as a movie, as construction, you can begin to pay attention to film form, as already suggested— the quality of the actors' performances, the cinematography, the sound design, and so on. If it is a well-made movie, there is a particular pleasure in responding to such aesthetic dimensions. Kubrick's *The Shining*, for example, makes for excellent distant viewing because

Figure 9.2 You can keep your horror-movie-induced fear in check by reminding yourself that it's just a movie, as suggested by the poster for the rape-revenge horror flick *Last House on the Left* (Sean S. Cunningham Films/Night Company/Lobster Enterprises, directed by Wes Craven, 1972). Such a strategy may even prompt you to enjoy the movie more.

the movie is so carefully and intelligently constructed. The set design and cinematography are simply otherworldly.

Play Tetris

Here is my final bit of advice, which I am stealing from the cognitive scientist Jim Davies: "If you don't want nightmares after you watch a scary movie," says Davies, "play some Tetris."[29] Why would that work? Well, scientists have found that playing Tetris right after a mildly traumatic experience can actually prevent post-traumatic stress disorder symptoms such as involuntary flashbacks. The idea is that the haunting images from a scary movie will not be as strongly encoded in memory if you fill your mind with something else right after watching, and Tetris is really good at mobilizing or even monopolizing your cognitive resources. Your mind will be so busy rotating those colored bricks that it will not have any leftover resources for forming strong memories of scary scenes. (If you are already an avid Tetris player, you will be familiar with the "Tetris effect"—the phenomenon where you start seeing colored tiles falling into place as soon as you close your eyes after a serious Tetris session, or start wondering how cereal boxes on a supermarket shelf might be rearranged to fill empty spaces and eliminate rows.)

In one study, participants watched a nasty 12-minute movie with real scenes of injury and death.[30] They then rested for half an hour. Next, half the participants played Tetris for 10 minutes, and the other half did nothing. As it turns out, those who had played Tetris had significantly fewer PTSD symptoms, including flashbacks, over the next week—the Tetris players had about a third of the flashback memories suffered by the nonplayers. The researchers think that playing Tetris works as a kind of "cognitive vaccine" against traumatic memories, and they suggest that there is a six-hour window to disrupt memory consolidation. So even if you disregard my advice against watching a horror movie in a movie theater, you still have time to get home and cognitively vaccinate yourself against nightmares and flashbacks with a session of Tetris.

Remind Me, Why Would I Wanna Watch That Stuff?

At this point you may be thinking: "That sounds like an awful lot of trouble to avoid being psychologically hurt by a movie that I don't particularly want to see, and that nobody is asking me to see." Well, yes, but the pleasures of horror are substantial and manifold. Otherwise horror would not be such a perennially popular genre. Of course, horror is not for everybody, and you may have made it this far in the book without feeling the slightest urge to watch a scary movie. I will try not to belabor the point, but I would like to say a bit more about the pleasures and benefits of horror before we part ways.

A really good horror movie takes you out of yourself—makes you forget your troubles and concerns for about 90 minutes—and simultaneously brings you into contact with your own body in a state of arousal and your own emotions at high intensity. Your mood may be improved. You get to vicariously experience amazing and terrifying things while in perfect safety, and you may even be moved by the aesthetic qualities of the movie. If it is an intelligent horror movie, you may be intellectually challenged. Your moral sense will be mobilized and perhaps subtly recalibrated. You may learn about psychological and social phenomena—the depths of despair, the heights of courage in the face of evil, the many ways relationships can be corrupted. You can confront anxieties—your own and those that permeate your culture. And finally, you may have an intensely social experience—one that bonds you and your co-viewers. Sharing an experience amplifies it, as we have seen, and sharing an experience brings individuals together—that goes for humans, for chimpanzees, even for *fish*, it is such a basic biological phenomenon.[31]

A fun study published in 1989 observed couples as they entered and left the cinema.[32] One group of couples went to see a documentary, while another group of couples went to see a suspense thriller— a "high-arousal" movie about "blackmail and murder." (The movie is called *52 Pick-Up* and came out in 1986.) The researchers, who were hiding outside the cinema, kept track of how much the cinemagoers talked to each other and how frequently they touched each other. For the couples who went to see the documentary, there was no change in affiliative behavior before and after the movie. For the couples who went to see the movie about blackmail and murder, however, the researchers observed significantly more affiliative behavior as they were leaving the movie theater. Now, *52 Pick-Up* is not a bona fide horror movie, but from my own observations, a similar principle applies. Horror brings us together.

On that note, I would like to wish you luck as you enter the dark and wonderful world of horror cinema. The grumpy German philosopher Nietzsche warned people against staring into the abyss for too long, but never mind that. There is a lot of fun to be had, staring into the abyss on the screen. It may even be good for you. As the old chestnut has it, that which doesn't kill you, makes you stronger. (That was Nietzsche too, by the way.)

Acknowledgments

Thanks to my brilliant editor at Oxford University Press, Norman Hirschy. I am grateful for Norm's faith in me (he is the one who suggested that I write this book), and for his unwavering helpfulness throughout the process of converting idea to book.

Thanks to Coltan Scrivner for reading and insightfully commenting on the whole manuscript; to my two research interns, Katrine Dahl Sørensen and Marie Søndergaard, for also going over the whole book and giving valuable feedback, and to Marc Hye-Knudsen for terrific research assistance. Thanks to Catherine Lester for providing vital feedback on the chapter on kids and horror and for helping me with suggestions for child-friendly scary movies. Anybody interested in the subject should check out Cat's wonderful new book, *Horror Films for Children* (2021). Thanks, also, to the three anonymous peer-reviewers who each offered helpful advice and constructive criticism. And a special thanks to my friend and colleague Jens Kjeldgaard-Christiansen. Jens's research expertise is villains, which is a bit ironic since he's such an all-round good guy himself. He patiently read, reread, and sometimes re-reread the chapter drafts that I sent him. The book is much stronger for his input.

Thanks to my family for being there, and a special thanks to my daughter Laura for diligently collecting data on horror movie production; my son Tobias for playing horror video games with me; my wife Camilla for sticking with me and my creepy research interests and for being who she is (sharp, witty, and hot as ever), and our dog Ponyo for fearlessly accompanying me on spooky late-night thinking-walks.

Thanks to my collaborators—in particular Marc Malmdorf Andersen, Brian Boutwell, Joseph Carroll, Marc Hye-Knudsen, John A. Johnson, Emelie Jonsson, Jens Kjeldgaard-Christiansen, Victoria

McCollum, Todd Platts, Uffe Schjoedt, and Coltan Scrivner—for excellent projects, several of which are discussed in this book. Thanks to the various funding agencies that have supported the research, in particular the seed funding program at the Interacting Minds Centre, Aarhus University, and the Independent Research Fund Denmark (grant number 0132-00204B).

Finally, thanks as ever to my friend Mike for introducing me to the wonders of horror cinema a quarter of a century ago, and to all the awesome horror artists out there—directors, writers, programmers, designers, and so on—without whom the world would be a less scary place, but also a much less fun place.

Notes

Preface

1. R. Nicholas Carleton, "Fear of the Unknown: One Fear to Rule Them All?," *Journal of Anxiety Disorders* 41 (2016), https://doi.org/http://dx.doi.org/10.1016/j.janxdis.2016.03.011.
2. Guillermo del Toro, "Haunted Castles, Dark Mirrors: On the Penguin Horror Series," ed. S. T. Joshi, *The Thing on the Doorstep and Other Weird Stories* (New York: Penguin, 2013), 1.

Chapter 1

1. David M. Buss, ed., *The Handbook of Evolutionary Psychology*, 2nd ed. (Hoboken, NJ: John Wiley & Sons, 2016).
2. Joseph Carroll, "Imagination, the Brain's Default Mode Network, and Imaginative Verbal Artifacts," in *Evolutionary Perspectives on Imaginative Culture*, ed. Joseph Carroll, Mathias Clasen, and Emelie Jonsson (New York: Springer, 2020), 31–52; Valerie van Mulukom, "The Evolution of Imagination and Fiction through Generativity and Narrative," in Carroll, Clasen, and Jonsson, *Evolutionary Perspectives on Imaginative Culture*, 53–70.
3. Peter Wühr, Benjamin P. Lange, and Sascha Schwarz, "Tears or Fears? Comparing Gender Stereotypes about Movie Preferences to Actual Preferences," *Frontiers in Psychology* 8 (2017), https://doi.org/10.3389/fpsyg.2017.00428.
4. Cynthia A. Hoffner and Kenneth J. Levine, "Enjoyment of Mediated Fright and Violence: A Meta-analysis," *Media Psychology* 7, no. 2 (2005), https://doi.org/10.1207/S1532785XMEP0702_5; G. Neil Martin, "(Why) Do You Like Scary Movies? A Review of the Empirical Research on Psychological Responses to Horror Films," *Frontiers in Psychology* 10 (2019), https://doi.org/10.3389/fpsyg.2019.02298; Stephen Follows, *The Horror Report* (n.p.: Film Data Fund, 2017), 120.
5. Mathias Clasen, Jens Kjeldgaard-Christiansen, and John A. Johnson, "Horror, Personality, and Threat Simulation: A Survey on the Psychology of Scary Media," *Evolutionary Behavioral Sciences* 14, no. 3 (2020), https://doi.org/10.1037/ebs0000152.

6. Anne Campbell, "Survival, Selection, and Sex Differences in Fear," in *The Cambridge Handbook of Evolutionary Perspectives on Human Behavior*, ed. Lance Workman, Will Reader, and Jerome H. Barkow (Cambridge: Cambridge University Press, 2020).

7. Laith Al-Shawaf, David M. G. Lewis, and David M. Buss, "Sex Differences in Disgust: Why Are Women More Easily Disgusted Than Men?," *Emotion Review* 10, no. 2 (2017), https://doi.org/10.1177/1754073917709940.

8. Clasen, Kjeldgaard-Christiansen, and Johnson, "Horror, Personality."

9. Follows, *The Horror Report*, 122.

10. Hoffner and Levine, "Enjoyment of Mediated Fright."

11. Viktória Tamás et al., "The Young Male Syndrome—an Analysis of Sex, Age, Risk Taking and Mortality in Patients with Severe Traumatic Brain Injuries," *Frontiers in Neurology* 10 (2019), https://doi.org/10.3389/fneur.2019.00366.

12. Tom Robinson, Clark Callahan, and Keith Evans, "Why Do We Keep Going Back? A Q Method Analysis of Our Attraction to Horror Movies," *Operant Subjectivity* 37, nos. 1–2 (2014).

13. Mathias Clasen, Marc Andersen, and Uffe Schjoedt, "Adrenaline Junkies and White-Knucklers: A Quantitative Study of Fear Management in Haunted House Visitors," *Poetics* 73 (2019), https://doi.org/10.1016/j.poetic.2019.01.002.

14. Follows, *The Horror Report*, 172.

15. Murray Leeder, *Horror Film: A Critical Introduction* (New York: Bloomsbury Academic, 2018).

16. Aristotle, *Poetics*, trans. Malcolm Heath (New York: Penguin, 1997).

17. Catherine Clepper, "'Death by Fright': Risk, Consent, and Evidentiary Objects in William Castle's Rigged Houses," *Film History* 28, no. 3 (2016), https://doi.org/10.2979/filmhistory.28.3.04.

18. Mathias Clasen, *Why Horror Seduces* (New York: Oxford University Press, 2017).

19. Arne Öhman and Susan Mineka, "Fears, Phobias, and Preparedness: Toward an Evolved Module of Fear and Fear Learning," *Psychological Review* 108, no. 3 (2001), http://www.ncbi.nlm.nih.gov/pubmed/11488376.

20. Randolph M. Nesse, "The Smoke Detector Principle," *Annals of the New York Academy of Sciences* 935, no. 1 (2006), https://doi.org/10.1111/j.1749-6632.2001.tb03472.x.

21. Matthew Hudson et al., "Dissociable Neural Systems for Unconditioned Acute and Sustained Fear," *NeuroImage* 216 (2020), https://doi.org/10.1016/j.neuroimage.2020.116522.

22. Denis Dutton, *The Art Instinct: Beauty, Pleasure, & Human Evolution* (New York: Bloomsbury Press, 2009).

23. Raymond A. Mar and Keith Oatley, "The Function of Fiction Is the Abstraction and Simulation of Social Experience," *Perspectives on Psychological Science* 3, no. 3 (2008), https://doi.org/10.1111/j.1745-6924.2008.00073.x.

Chapter 2

1. Julian Hanich, *Cinematic Emotion in Horror Films and Thrillers: The Aesthetic Paradox of Pleasurable Fear* (New York: Routledge, 2010).

2. Robert Baird, "The Startle Effect: Implications for Spectator Cognition and Media Theory," *Film Quarterly* 53, no. 3 (2000), https://doi.org/10.1525/fq.2000.53.3.04a00030; Murray Smith, *Film, Art, and the Third Culture: A Naturalized Aesthetics of Film* (Oxford: Oxford University Press, 2017), 92–98; Xavier Aldana Reyes, *Horror Film and Affect: Towards a Corporeal Model of Viewership* (New York: Routledge, 2016), 150–62.

3. Baird, "Startle Effect," 23 n. 10.

4. Baird, "Startle Effect," 15.

5. Christian Grillon et al., "Fear-Potentiated Startle in Humans: Effects of Anticipatory Anxiety on the Acoustic Blink Reflex," *Psychophysiology* 28, no. 5 (1991), https://doi.org/10.1111/j.1469-8986.1991.tb01999.x.

6. Ronald C. Simons, *Boo! Culture, Experience, and the Startle Reflex* (New York: Oxford University Press, 1996), 14.

7. Hanich, *Cinematic Emotion*, 136.

8. Valerio Sbravatti, "Acoustic Startles in Horror Films: A Neurofilmological Approach," *Projections* 13, no. 1 (2019): 45–66.

9. Sbravatti, "Acoustic Startles."

10. Daniel T. Blumstein, Richard Davitian, and Peter D. Kaye, "Do Film Soundtracks Contain Nonlinear Analogues to Influence Emotion?," *Biology Letters* 6, no. 6 (2010), https://doi.org/10.1098/rsbl.2010.0333.

11. Claude Alain, James Bigelow, and Amy Poremba, "Achilles' Ear? Inferior Human Short-Term and Recognition Memory in the Auditory Modality," *PLoS ONE* 9, no. 2 (2014), https://doi.org/10.1371/journal.pone.0089914.

12. Simons, *Boo*, 8.

13. Jenefer Robinson, "Startle," *Journal of Philosophy* 92, no. 2 (1995): 54–55, https://doi.org/10.2307/2940940.

14. Jinhee Choi, "Fits and Startles: Cognitivism Revisited," *Journal of Aesthetics and Art Criticism* 61, no. 2 (2003), https://doi.org/10.1111/1540-6245.00102.

15. Simons, *Boo*; Nico H. Frijda, *The Emotions* (Cambridge: Cambridge University Press, 1986).

16. Quoted in Robinson, "Startle," 55.

17. Peter J. Lang, Margaret M. Bradley, and Bruce N. Cuthbert, "Emotion, Attention, and the Startle Reflex," *Psychological Review* 97, no. 3 (1990), https://doi.org/10.1037/0033-295x.97.3.377.

18. Simons, *Boo*, 22.

19. Quoted in Robinson, "Startle," 57.

20. Choi, "Fits and Startles," 150.

21. Simons, *Boo*.

22. Marvin Zuckerman, *Behavioral Expressions and Biosocial Bases of Sensation Seeking* (New York: Cambridge University Press, 1994).

23. Baird, "Startle Effect," 13.

24. "Do Modern Horror Movies Contain More Jump Scares Than Older Movies?," HacShac, 2020, accessed July 24, 2020, https://wheresthejump.com/do-modern-horror-movies-contain-more-jump-scares-than-older-movies/.

25. Seung-Schik Yoo et al., "The Human Emotional Brain without Sleep—A Prefrontal Amygdala Disconnect," *Current Biology* 17, no. 20 (2007), https://doi.org/10.1016/j.cub.2007.08.007.

26. Simons, *Boo*, 14.

27. Christian Grillon et al., "Mental Fatigue Impairs Emotion Regulation," *Emotion* 15, no. 3 (2015), https://doi.org/10.1037/emo0000058.

28. Simons, *Boo*, 12; Werner G. K. Stritzke, Christopher J. Patrick, and Alan R. Lang, "Alcohol and Human Emotion: A Multidimensional Analysis Incorporating Startle-Probe Methodology," *Journal of Abnormal Psychology* 104, no. 1 (1995), https://doi.org/10.1037/0021-843x.104.1.114.

29. Simons, *Boo*, 14; C. Grillon and M. Davis, "Fear-Potentiated Startle Conditioning in Humans: Explicit and Contextual Cue Conditioning Following Paired versus Unpaired Training," *Psychophysiology* 34, no. 4 (July 1997), http://www.ncbi.nlm.nih.gov/pubmed/9260498.

30. Sbravatti, "Acoustic Startles," 57.

31. Hanich, *Cinematic Emotion*, 139–41.

32. Clasen, Andersen, and Schjoedt, "Adrenaline Junkies."

33. Hanich, *Cinematic Emotion*, 64–65; Ed S. Tan, *Emotion and the Structure of Narrative Film: Film as an Emotion Machine* (Hillsdale, NJ: Lawrence Erlbaum, 1996).

Chapter 3

1. Jason Zinoman, *Shock Value: How a Few Eccentric Outsiders Gave Us Nightmares, Conquered Hollywood, and Invented Modern Horror* (New York: Penguin, 2011), 101–2.

2. Judy Klemesrud, "They Wait Hours—to Be Shocked," *New York Times*, January 27, 1974, https://www.nytimes.com/1974/01/27/archives/they-wait-hoursto-be-shocked-the-exorcist-got-mixed-reviews-why-has.html.

3. "Exorcist Fever," *Time*, February 11, 1974.

4. James C. Bozzuto, "Cinematic Neurosis Following 'The Exorcist': Report of Four Cases," *Journal of Nervous and Mental Disease* 161, no. 1 (1975), https://doi.org/10.1097/00005053-197507000-00005.

5. Bruce Ballon and Molyn Leszcz, "Horror Films: Tales to Master Terror or Shapers of Trauma?," *American Journal of Psychotherapy* 61, no. 2 (2007), https://doi.org/10.1176/appi.psychotherapy.2007.61.2.211.

6. Ballon and Leszcz, "Horror Films," 212.

7. D. Simons and W. R. Silveira, "Post-traumatic Stress Disorder in Children after Television Programmes," *British Medical Journal* 308, no. 6925 (1994), https://doi.org/10.1136/bmj.308.6925.389.

8. Rebecca Woods, "*Ghostwatch*: The BBC Spoof That Duped a Nation," *BBC News*, October 30, 2017, https://www.bbc.com/news/uk-england-41740176.

9. Ballon and Leszcz, "Horror Films."

10. Joanne Cantor, "Fright Reactions to Mass Media," in *Media Effects: Advances in Theory and Research*, ed. Jennings Bryant and Mary Beth Oliver (New York: Routledge, 2009), 287–303.

11. Glenn G. Sparks, "The Prevalence and Intensity of Fright Reactions to Mass Media: Implications of the Activation-Arousal View," *Communication Quarterly* 37, no. 2 (1989): 113, https://doi.org/10.1080/01463378909385532.

12. Kristen Harrison and Joanne Cantor, "Tales from the Screen: Enduring Fright Reactions to Scary Media," *Media Psychology* 1, no. 2 (1999), https://doi.org/10.1207/s1532785xmep0102_1.

13. Joanne Cantor, "'I'll Never Have a Clown in My House'—Why Movie Horror Lives On," *Poetics Today* 25, no. 2 (2004): 288, http://muse.jhu.edu/journals/poetics_today/v025/25.2cantor.html.

14. Martin, "(Why) Do You Like Scary Movies."

15. Sparks, "Prevalence and Intensity."

16. Dolf Zillmann and James B. Weaver III, "Gender-Socialization Theory of Reactions to Horror," in *Horror Films: Current Research on Audience Preferences and Reactions*, ed. James B. Weaver III and Ron Tamborini (New York: Routledge, 1996), 81–101.

17. Martin, "(Why) Do You Like Scary Movies," 13.

18. Roger Ebert, "The Exorcist," *Chicago Sun-Times*, 1973, https://www.rogerebert.com/reviews/the-exorcist-1973.

19. Val Curtis, Robert Aunger, and Tamer Rabie, "Evidence That Disgust Evolved to Protect from Risk of Disease," *Proceedings of the Royal Society of London B: Biological Sciences* 271, Suppl 4 (2004), https://doi.org/10.1098/rsbl.2003.0144.

20. Joshua M. Tybur et al., "Disgust: Evolved Function and Structure," *Psychological Review* 120, no. 1 (2013), https://doi.org/10.1037/a0030778.

21. John Sanford, "Blood, Sweat and Fears: A Common Phobia's Odd Pathophysiology," *Stanford Medicine* (2013). http://sm.stanford.edu/archive/stanmed/2013spring/article6.html.

22. Hans Kruuk, *Hunter and Hunted: Relationships between Carnivores and People* (Cambridge: Cambridge University Press, 2002).

23. Coltan Scrivner, "Psychology of Morbid Curiosity: Development and Initial Validation of the Morbid Curiosity Scale" (2020), accessed February 6, 2021, https://psyarxiv.com/xug34/.

24. Coltan Scrivner, "An Infectious Curiosity: Morbid Curiosity and Media Preferences during a Pandemic," *Evolutionary Studies in Imaginative Culture* 5, no. 1 (2020), https://doi.org/10.26613/esic/5.1.206.

25. Michael A. Arnzen, "Who's Laughing Now? The Postmodern Splatter Film," *Journal of Popular Film and Television* 21, no. 4 (1994), https://doi.org/10.1080/01956051.1994.9943985.

26. Carl Plantinga, "The Scene of Empathy and the Human Face on Film," in *Passionate Views: Film, Cognition, and Emotion*, ed. Carl Plantinga and Greg M. Smith (Baltimore: Johns Hopkins University Press, 1999), 239–55.

27. Aldana Reyes, *Horror Film and Affect*.

28. James S. Nairne, Sarah R. Thompson, and Josefa N. S. Pandeirada, "Adaptive Memory: Survival Processing Enhances Retention," *Journal of Experimental Psychology: Learning, Memory, and Cognition* 33, no. 2 (2007), https://doi.org/10.1037/0278-7393.33.2.263.

29. Patrick Bonin et al., "'In Your Head, Zombie': Zombies, Predation and Memory," *Journal of Cognitive Psychology* 31, no. 7 (2019), https://doi.org/10.1080/20445911.2019.1664557; Stephanie A. Kazanas and Jeanette Altarriba, "Did Our Ancestors Fear the Unknown? The Role of Predation in the Survival Advantage," *Evolutionary Behavioral Sciences* 11, no. 1 (2017), https://doi.org/10.1037/ebs0000074.

30. Joseph M. Stubbersfield, Emma G. Flynn, and Jamshid J. Tehrani, "Cognitive Evolution and the Transmission of Popular Narratives: A Literature Review and Application to Urban Legends," *Evolutionary Studies in Imaginative Culture* 1, no. 1 (2018), https://doi.org/10.26613/esic/1.1.20.

31. "The Exorcist," *Variety*, December 31, 1973, https://variety.com/1972/film/reviews/the-exorcist-2-1200422937/.

32. Van Mulukom, "Evolution of Imagination."

33. Clasen, Kjeldgaard-Christiansen, and Johnson, "Horror, Personality."

34. Linda Williams, "Film Bodies: Gender, Genre, and Excess," *Film Quarterly* 44, no. 4 (1991), https://doi.org/10.2307/1212758, www.jstor.org/stable/1212758.

35. Joseph Carroll, "Death in Literature," in *Evolutionary Perspectives on Death*, ed. Todd K. Shackelford and Virgil Zeigler-Hill (New York: Springer, 2019), 137–59.

36. Aldana Reyes, *Horror Film and Affect*, 1.

37. Virginie Sterpenich et al., "Fear in Dreams and in Wakefulness: Evidence for Day/Night Affective Homeostasis," *Human Brain Mapping* 41, no. 3 (2019), https://doi.org/10.1002/hbm.24843.

38. Jordan Crucchiola, "What Makes the New Horror Film *It Follows* So Damn Good," *Wired*, March 17, 2015, https://www.wired.com/2015/03/it-follows-unholy-trinity/.

39. Craig Marks and Rob Tannenbaum, "Freddy Lives: An Oral History of *A Nightmare on Elm Street*," *Vulture*, October 20, 2014, https://www.vulture.com/2014/10/nightmare-on-elm-street-oral-history.html.

40. Wayne King, "Nightmares Suspected in Bed Deaths of 18 Laotians," *New York Times*, May 10, 1981, https://www.nytimes.com/1981/05/10/us/nightmares-suspected-in-bed-deaths-of-18-laotians.html.

41. Antti Revonsuo, "The Reinterpretation of Dreams: An Evolutionary Hypothesis of the Function of Dreaming," *Behavioral and Brain Sciences* 23, no. 6 (2000), http://www.ncbi.nlm.nih.gov/pubmed/11515147.

42. Katja Valli and Antti Revonsuo, "The Threat Simulation Theory in Light of Recent Empirical Evidence: A Review," *American Journal of Psychology* 122, no. 1 (2009), http://www.ncbi.nlm.nih.gov/pubmed/19353929.

43. Steven J. Hoekstra, Richard Jackson Harris, and Angela L. Helmick, "Autobiographical Memories about the Experience of Seeing Frightening Movies in Childhood," *Media Psychology* 1, no. 2 (1999): 117, https://doi.org/10.1207/s1532785xmep0102_2.

44. Carroll E. Izard, *Human Emotions* (New York: Plenum Press, 1977), 355.

45. Clasen, Kjeldgaard-Christiansen, and Johnson, "Horror, Personality."

46. Marc Malmdorf Andersen et al., "Playing with Fear: A Field Study in Recreational Horror," *Psychological Science* 31, no. 12 (2020): 1497–512, https://doi.org/10.1177/0956797620972116.

47. Woods, "*Ghostwatch.*"

48. Margee Kerr, Greg J. Siegle, and Jahala Orsini, "Voluntary Arousing Negative Experiences (VANE): Why We Like to Be Scared," *Emotion* 19, no. 4 (2019), https://doi.org/10.1037/emo0000470.

49. Clasen, Kjeldgaard-Christiansen, and Johnson, "Horror, Personality."

50. Dimitris Xygalatas et al., "Extreme Rituals Promote Prosociality," *Psychological Science* 24, no. 8 (2013), https://doi.org/10.1177/0956797612472910.

51. Brock Bastian, Jolanda Jetten, and Laura J. Ferris, "Pain as Social Glue," *Psychological Science* 25, no. 11 (2014), https://doi.org/10.1177/0956797614545886.

52. Richard Nowell, *Blood Money: A History of the First Teen Slasher Film Cycle* (New York: Continuum, 2011).

53. Nowell, *Blood Money*, 35.

54. Richard Jackson Harris et al., "Young Men's and Women's Different Autobiographical Memories of the Experience of Seeing Frightening Movies on a Date," *Media Psychology* 2, no. 3 (2000), https://doi.org/10.1207/s1532785xmep0203_3.

55. Donald G. Dutton and Arthur P. Aron, "Some Evidence for Heightened Sexual Attraction under Conditions of High Anxiety," *Journal of Personality and Social Psychology* 30, no. 4 (1974), https://doi.org/10.1037/h0037031.

56. Dolf Zillmann et al., "Effects of an Opposite-Gender Companion's Affect to Horror on Distress, Delight, and Attraction," *Journal of Personality and Social Psychology* 51, no. 3 (1986), https://doi.org/10.1037/0022-3514.51.3.586.

57. Zillmann and Weaver, "Gender-Socialization Theory," 95.

58. Christian Rudder, "The Best Questions for a First Date," *OkCupid*, April 29, 2011, https://theblog.okcupid.com/the-best-questions-for-a-first-date-dba6adaa9df2.

59. Clasen, Andersen, and Schjoedt, "Adrenaline Junkies."

60. Coltan Scrivner et al., "Pandemic Practice: Horror Fans and Morbidly Curious Individuals Are More Psychologically Resilient during the COVID-19 Pandemic," *Personality and Individual Differences* 168 (2021), https://doi.org/10.1016/j.paid.2020.110397.

61. Abby Moss, "Why Some Anxious People Find Comfort in Horror Movies," *Vice*, November 8, 2017, https://www.vice.com/en_us/article/a3wdzk/why-some-anxious-people-find-comfort-in-horror-movies.

62. Caroline Bologna, "Why Some People with Anxiety Love Watching Horror Movies," *Huffington Post*, October 31, 2019, https://www.huffpost.com/entry/anxiety-love-watching-horror-movies_l_5d277587e4b02a5a5d57b59e.

63. Tiffany Simone, "The Power of Horror Films as a Cure for Anxiety," *Medium.com*, July 22, 2018, https://medium.com/@tiffanysdillon/the-power-of-horror-films-as-cure-for-anxiety-e30830e0c2b1.

Chapter 4

1. *Subliminal Communication Technology: Hearing before the Subcommittee on Transportation, Aviation and Materials of the Committee on Science and Technology, U.S. House of Representatives, Ninety-Eighth Congress, Second Session* (Washington, DC: US Government Printing Office, 1984), 1084 n. 42, https://books.google.dk/books?id=vjosAAAAMAAJ.

2. R. E. Noble, "Stephen King Wrist," *Western Journal of Medicine* 171, no. 2 (1999): 80.

3. Aldana Reyes, *Horror Film and Affect*.

4. Hanich, *Cinematic Emotion*.

5. Walter B. Cannon, *Bodily Changes in Pain, Hunger, Fear and Rage: An Account of Recent Researches into the Function of Emotional Excitement* (New York: D. Appleton, 1915).

6. Walter B. Cannon, "'Voodoo' Death," *American Anthropologist* 44, no. 2 (1942), https://doi.org/10.1525/aa.1942.44.2.02a00010.

7. Esther M. Sternberg, "Walter B. Cannon and '"Voodoo" Death': A Perspective from 60 Years on," *American Journal of Public Health* 92, no. 10 (2002), https://doi.org/10.2105/ajph.92.10.1564.

8. Frederick Manson, "Notes of a Case of Death from Fright," *The Lancet* 48, no. 1213 (1846), https://doi.org/10.1016/s0140-6736(02)89361-8.

9. "Student Dies of Shock While Watching Horror Films," *Times of India* (Hyderabad), December 6, 2010, https://timesofindia.indiatimes.com/city/hyderabad/Student-dies-of-shock-while-watching-horror-films/articleshow/7049952.cms.

10. "65-Yr-Old Dies While Watching Horror Movie," *Times of India* (Chennai), June 17, 2016, https://timesofindia.indiatimes.com/city/chennai/65-yr-old-dies-while-watching-horror-movie/articleshow/52792653.cms.

11. "Watching Horror Films Burns Nearly 200 Calories a Time," *The Telegraph* (London), October 28, 2012, https://www.telegraph.co.uk/news/uknews/9638876/Watching-horror-films-burns-nearly-200-calories-a-time.html.

12. Joseph Cools, David E. Schotte, and Richard J. McNally, "Emotional Arousal and Overeating in Restrained Eaters," *Journal of Abnormal Psychology* 101, no. 2 (1992), https://doi.org/10.1037/0021-843x.101.2.348.

13. Rubina Mian et al., "Observing a Fictitious Stressful Event: Haematological Changes, Including Circulating Leukocyte Activation," *Stress* 6, no. 1 (2009), https://doi.org/10.1080/1025389031000101349.

14. Banne Nemeth et al., "Bloodcurdling Movies and Measures of Coagulation: Fear Factor Crossover Trial," *BMJ* (2015), bmj.h6367 https://doi.org/10.1136/bmj.h6367.

15. Dimitris Xygalatas et al., "Effects of Extreme Ritual Practices on Psychophysiological Well-Being," *Current Anthropology* 60, no. 5 (2019), https://doi.org/10.1086/705665.

16. Xygalatas et al., "Effects of Extreme Ritual Practices," 706.

Chapter 5

1. David Hajdu, *The Ten-Cent Plague: The Great Comic-Book Scare and How It Changed America* (New York: Farrar, Straus and Giroux, 2008).

2. Christopher J. Ferguson, *Adolescents, Crime, and the Media: A Critical Analysis* (New York: Springer, 2013).

3. David Edelstein, "Now Playing at Your Local Multiplex: Torture Porn," *New York Magazine*, January 26, 2006, https://nymag.com/movies/features/15622/.

4. Aaron Kerner, *Torture Porn in the Wake of 9/11: Horror, Exploitation, and the Cinema of Sensation* (New Brunswick, NJ: Rutgers University Press, 2015).

5. Kira Cochrane, "For Your Entertainment," *The Guardian* (London), May 1, 2007, https://www.theguardian.com/film/2007/may/01/gender.world.

6. Lenore Skenazy, "It's Torture! It's Porn! What's Not to Like? Plenty, Actually," *AdAge*, May 28, 2007, https://adage.com/article/lenore-skenazy/torture-porn-plenty/116897.

7. Gianluca Di Muzio, "The Immorality of Horror Films," *International Journal of Applied Philosophy* 20, no. 2 (2006), https://doi.org/10.5840/ijap200620222.

8. Marius A. Pascale, "Art Horror, Reactive Attitudes, and Compassionate Slashers," *International Journal of Applied Philosophy* 33, no. 1 (2019), https://doi.org/10.5840/ijap201981116.

9. Steve Jones, *Torture Porn: Popular Horror after Saw* (London: Palgrave Macmillan, 2013).

10. Blair Davis and Kial Natale, "'The Pound of Flesh Which I Demand,'" in *American Horror Film: The Genre at the Turn of the Millennium*, ed. Steffen Hantke (Jackson: University Press of Mississippi, 2010), 35–56.

11. "Eli Roth Talks Hostel: Part II, the Internet, the MPAA and More," *Movieweb*, 2007, accessed August 2, 2020, https://movieweb.com/eli-roth-talks-hostel-part-ii-the-internet-the-mpaa-and-more/.

12. Isabel C. Pinedo, "Torture Porn," in *A Companion to the Horror Film*, ed. Harry M. Benshoff (Hoboken, NJ: John Wiley & Sons, 2014), 359.

13. Todd K. Platts and Mathias Clasen, "Scary Business: Horror at the North American Box Office, 2006–2016," *Frames Cinema Journal*, no. 11 (2017), http://framescinemajournal.com/article/scary-business-horror-at-the-north-american-box-office-2006-2016/.

14. Martin Barker, "The UK 'Video Nasties' Campaign Revisited: Panics, Claims-Making, Risks, and Politics," in *Discourses of Anxiety over Childhood and Youth across Cultures*, ed. Liza Tsaliki and Despina Chronaki (Cham: Springer, 2020).

15. Julian Petley, "'Are We Insane?' The 'Video Nasty' Moral Panic," *Recherches sociologiques et anthropologiques* 43, no. 1 (2012), https://doi.org/10.4000/rsa.839.

16. Laurence Phelan, "Film Censorship: How Moral Panic Led to a Mass Ban of 'Video Nasties,'" *The Independent* (London), July 13, 2015, https://www.independent.co.uk/arts-entertainment/films/features/film-censorship-how-moral-panic-led-to-a-mass-ban-of-video-nasties-9600998.html.

17. Terry Kirby, "Video Link to Bulger Murder Disputed," *The Independent* (London), November 26, 1993, https://www.independent.co.uk/news/video-link-to-bulger-murder-disputed-1506766.html.

18. Gene Siskel and Roger Ebert, *Sneak Previews with Siskel and Ebert* (Public Broadcasting System, 1980), October 24.

19. Richard Nowell, "'There's More Than One Way to Lose Your Heart': The American Film Industry, Early Teen Slasher Films, and Female Youth," *Cinema Journal* 51, no. 1 (2011): 115–40.

20. A. Dana Ménard, Angela Weaver, and Christine Cabrera, "'There Are Certain Rules That One Must Abide By': Predictors of Mortality in Slasher

Films," *Sexuality & Culture* 23, no. 2 (2019), https://doi.org/10.1007/s12119-018-09583-2.

21. Marc Hye-Knudsen and Mathias Clasen, "'So-Bad-It's-Good': The Room and the Paradoxical Appeal of Bad Films," *16:9*, November 28, 2019, http://www.16-9.dk/2019/11/so-bad-its-good/.

22. "Report of the Media Violence Commission," *Aggressive Behavior* 38, no. 5 (2012), https://doi.org/10.1002/ab.21443.

23. Christopher J. Ferguson, "Does Media Violence Predict Societal Violence? It Depends on What You Look At and When," *Journal of Communication* 65, no. 1 (2015), https://doi.org/10.1111/jcom.12129.

24. Gordon Dahl and Stefano DellaVigna, "Does Movie Violence Increase Violent Crime?," *Quarterly Journal of Economics* 124, no. 2 (2009), https://doi.org/10.1162/qjec.2009.124.2.677.

25. Dahl and DellaVigna, "Does Movie Violence Increase Violent Crime?," 667.

26. Patrick M. Markey, Juliana E. French, and Charlotte N. Markey, "Violent Movies and Severe Acts of Violence: Sensationalism versus Science," *Human Communication Research* 41, no. 2 (2015), https://doi.org/10.1111/hcre.12046.

27. Raul A. Ramos et al., "Comfortably Numb or Just Yet Another Movie? Media Violence Exposure Does Not Reduce Viewer Empathy for Victims of Real Violence among Primarily Hispanic Viewers," *Psychology of Popular Media Culture* 2, no. 1 (2013), https://doi.org/10.1037/a0030119.

28. Joseph Carroll et al., *Graphing Jane Austen: The Evolutionary Basis of Literary Meaning* (Basingstoke: Palgrave Macmillan, 2012).

29. Jens Kjeldgaard-Christiansen, "A Structure of Antipathy: Constructing the Villain in Narrative Film," *Projections* 13, no. 1 (2019), https://doi.org/10.3167/proj.2019.130105.

30. Allison Eden et al., "Perceptions of Moral Violations and Personality Traits among Heroes and Villains," *Mass Communication and Society* 18, no. 2 (2014), https://doi.org/10.1080/15205436.2014.923462.

31. Melanie C. Green, Timothy C. Brock, and Geoff F. Kaufman, "Understanding Media Enjoyment: The Role of Transportation into Narrative Worlds," *Communication Theory* 14, no. 4 (2004), https://doi.org/10.1111/j.1468-2885.2004.tb00317.x.

32. Mathias Clasen, "Hauntings of Human Nature: An Evolutionary Critique of King's *The Shining*," *Style* 51, no. 1 (2017): 76–88.

33. Daniel Smith et al., "Cooperation and the Evolution of Hunter-Gatherer Storytelling," *Nature Communications* 8, no. 1 (2017), https://doi.org/10.1038/s41467-017-02036-8.

34. Quoted in Kim Newman, *Nightmare Movies: Horror on Screen since the 1960s*, rev. ed. (London: Bloomsbury Publishing, 2011), 70.

35. Stephen King, *Danse Macabre* (New York: Berkley Books, 1983).

36. Robin Wood, "An Introduction to the American Horror Film," in *American Nightmare: Essays on the Horror Film*, ed. Andrew Britton et al. (Toronto: Festival of Festivals, 1979), 7–28.

37. David Andrews, "The Rape-Revenge Film: Biocultural Implications," *Jump Cut: A Review of Contemporary Media*, no. 54 (2012), http://www.ejumpcut.org/archive/jc54.2012/DAndrewsRapeRevenge/.

38. Andrews, "Rape-Revenge Film."

39. Mick Garris, *Post Mortem with Mick Garris*, podcast audio, 57: Joe Dante—Live from the 2019 Lucca Film Festival, 2019, https://www.stitcher.com/podcast/blumhouse/post-mortem-with-mick-garris/e/62018160.

Chapter 6

1. David J. Skal, *The Monster Show: A Cultural History of Horror*, rev. ed. (New York: Faber and Faber, 2001).

2. Stephen King, *Salem's Lot* (London: Hodder & Stoughton, 2008), 83.

3. Mick Garris, *Post Mortem with Mick Garris*, podcast audio, 90: Guillermo del Toro, 2020, https://www.stitcher.com/podcast/blumhouse/post-mortem-with-mick-garris/e/69782024.

4. Les Daniels, *Living in Fear: A History of Horror in the Mass Media* (New York: Da Capo Press, 1975); David Punter, *The Literature of Terror: A History of Gothic Fictions from 1765 to the Present Day*, 2 vols. (New York: Longman, 1996).

5. Mark Jancovich, "Genre and the Audience: Genre Classifications and Cultural Distinctions in the Mediation of *The Silence of the Lambs*," in *Horror, the Film Reader*, ed. Mark Jancovich (London: Routledge, 2002), 151–61.

6. Alishya Almeida, "*Parasite* as Horror Film," *Horror Homeroom*, July 7, 2020, http://www.horrorhomeroom.com/parasite-as-horror-film/.

7. Leeder, *Horror Film*, 138–41.

8. David Buckingham, *Moving Images: Understanding Children's Emotional Responses to Television* (Manchester: Manchester University Press, 1996), 98.

9. Steffen Hantke, "'They Don't Make 'Em Like They Used To': On the Rhetoric of Crisis and the Current State of American Horror Cinema," in Hantke, *American Horror Film*, vi–xiv.

10. Steve Rose, "How Post-Horror Movies Are Taking Over Cinema," *The Guardian* (London), July 6, 2017, https://www.theguardian.com/film/2017/jul/06/post-horror-films-scary-movies-ghost-story-it-comes-at-night.

11. Britt Hayes, "'Hereditary' Director Ari Aster on Why He Avoided Calling His Terrifying Debut a 'Horror Film,'" *ScreenCrush*, June 7, 2018, https://screencrush.com/ari-aster-interview-hereditary/.

12. Nicholas Barber, "Is Horror the Most Disrespected Genre?," *BBC Culture*, June 14, 2018, https://www.bbc.com/culture/article/20180614-is-horror-the-most-disrespected-genre.

13. Tom Nicholson, "The 2010s Were the Decade When Horror Got Smart," *Esquire*, December 20, 2019, https://www.esquire.com/uk/culture/film/a30284121/elevated-horror-2010s-peele-eggers-aster-blumhouse/.

14. Follows, *The Horror Report*, 113.

15. Theodore Sturgeon, "Books: On Hand," *Venture Science Fiction*, 1958, 66.

16. Follows, *The Horror Report*, 198.

17. "Annabelle Reviews—Metacritic," *Metacritic*, accessed August 2, 2020, https://www.metacritic.com/movie/annabelle.

18. Clasen, Kjeldgaard-Christiansen, and Johnson, "Horror, Personality."

19. Follows, *The Horror Report*, 120.

20. Ed Meza, "Guillermo del Toro on the Catholic Church, His Holy Trinity and Boris Karloff Epiphany," *Variety*, October 17, 2017, https://variety.com/2017/film/festivals/guillermo-del-toro-masterclass-2017-lumiere-festival-1202591885/.

21. Simons, *Boo*.

22. Douglas J. Lanska, "Jumping Frenchmen, Miryachit, and Latah: Culture-Specific Hyperstartle-Plus Syndromes," *Frontiers of Neurology and Neuroscience* 42 (2018): 122–31.

23. A. Peter McGraw and Caleb Warren, "Benign Violations: Making Immoral Behavior Funny," *Psychological Science* 21, no. 8 (2010), https://doi.org/10.1177/0956797610376073.

Chapter 7

1. Harrison and Cantor, "Tales from the Screen"; Maya Götz, Dafna Lemish, and Andrea Holler, *Fear in Front of the Screen: Children's Fears, Nightmares, and Thrills from TV* (Lanham, MD: Rowman & Littlefield, 2019).

2. Hoekstra, Harris, and Helmick, "Autobiographical Memories"; Joanne Cantor, *"Mommy, I'm Scared": How TV and Movies Frighten Children and What We Can Do to Protect Them* (Orlando, FL: Harcourt Brace, 1998).

3. Cantor, "Fright Reactions."

4. Barbara J. Wilson, "Media and Children's Aggression, Fear, and Altruism," *Future of Children* 18, no. 1 (2008): 103, https://doi.org/10.1353/foc.0.0005.

5. Hoekstra, Harris, and Helmick, "Autobiographical Memories."

6. Christina Clark and Amelia Foster, *Children's and Young People's Reading Habits and Preferences: The Who, What, Why, Where and When* (London: National Literacy Trust, 2005), 21, https://files.eric.ed.gov/fulltext/ED541603.pdf.

7. Buckingham, *Moving Images*, 98–99.

8. Edward L. Palmer, Anne B. Hockett, and Walter W. Dean, "The Television Family and Children's Fright Reactions," *Journal of Family Issues* 4, no. 2 (2016), https://doi.org/10.1177/019251383004002002.

9. Hoffner and Levine, "Enjoyment of Mediated Fright."

10. Catherine Lester, "The Children's Horror Film: Characterizing an 'Impossible' Subgenre," *Velvet Light Trap* 78 (2016), https://doi.org/10.7560/vlt7803.

11. Filipa Antunes, *Children Beware! Childhood, Horror and the PG-13 Rating* (Jefferson, NC: McFarland, 2020).

12. Lester, "Children's Horror Film," 24.

13. David F. Bjorklund and Anthony D. Pellegrini, *The Origins of Human Nature: Evolutionary Developmental Psychology* (Washington, DC: American Psychological Association, 2002); Deena S. Weisberg and Alison Gopnik, "Pretense, Counterfactuals, and Bayesian Causal Models: Why What Is Not Real Really Matters," *Cognitive Science* 37, no. 7 (2013), https://doi.org/10.1111/cogs.12069.

14. Francis F. Steen and Stephanie A. Owens, "Evolution's Pedagogy: An Adaptationist Model of Pretense and Entertainment," *Journal of Cognition and Culture* 1, no. 4 (2001).

15. Pascal Boyer and Brian Bergstrom, "Threat-Detection in Child Development: An Evolutionary Perspective," *Neuroscience & Biobehavioral Reviews* 35, no. 4 (2011), https://doi.org/10.1016/j.neubiorev.2010.08.010.

16. Joanne Cantor and Mary Beth Oliver, "Developmental Differences in Responses to Horror," in *Horror Films: Research on Audience Preference and Reactions*, ed. J. B. Weaver and R. Tamborini (Hillsdale, NJ: Lawrence Erlbaum Associates, Inc., Publishers, 1996), 63–80.

17. Cynthia Hoffner and Joanne Cantor, "Developmental Differences in Responses to a Television Character's Appearance and Behavior," *Developmental Psychology* 21, no. 6 (1985), https://doi.org/10.1037/0012-1649.21.6.1065.

18. Cantor, *Mommy, I'm Scared*, 57.

19. Jens Kjeldgaard-Christiansen and Sarah Helene Schmidt, "Disney's Shifting Visions of Villainy from the 1990s to the 2010s: A Biocultural Analysis," *Evolutionary Studies in Imaginative Culture* 3, no. 2 (2019), https://doi.org/10.26613/esic.3.2.140.

20. John C. Wright et al., "Young Children's Perceptions of Television Reality: Determinants and Developmental Differences," *Developmental Psychology* 30, no. 2 (1994), https://doi.org/10.1037/0012-1649.30.2.229.

21. Paul L. Harris et al., "Monsters, Ghosts and Witches: Testing the Limits of the Fantasy-Reality Distinction in Young Children," *British Journal of Developmental Psychology* 9, no. 1 (1991), https://doi.org/10.1111/j.2044-835X.1991.tb00865.x.

22. Deena Skolnick Weisberg et al., "Young Children are Reality-Prone When Thinking about Stories," *Journal of Cognition and Culture* 13, nos. 3–4 (2013), https://doi.org/10.1163/15685373-12342100.

23. Mark D. Seery, E. Alison Holman, and Roxane Cohen Silver, "Whatever Does Not Kill Us: Cumulative Lifetime Adversity, Vulnerability, and Resilience," *Journal of Personality and Social Psychology* 99, no. 6 (2010), https://doi.org/10.1037/a0021344.

24. Karen J. Parker et al., "Nonlinear Relationship between Early Life Stress Exposure and Subsequent Resilience in Monkeys," *Scientific Reports* 9, no. 1 (2019), https://doi.org/10.1038/s41598-019-52810-5.

25. Wilson, "Media and Children's Aggression."

26. M. Špinka, R. C. Newberry, and M. Bekoff, "Mammalian Play: Training for the Unexpected," *Quarterly Review of Biology* 76, no. 2 (2001).

27. Wilson, "Media and Children's Aggression," 110.

28. Joanne Cantor and Barbara J. Wilson, "Modifying Fear Responses to Mass Media in Preschool and Elementary School Children," *Journal of Broadcasting* 28, no. 4 (2009), https://doi.org/10.1080/08838158409386552.

29. Cantor and Wilson, "Modifying Fear Responses," 436.

30. Barbara J. Wilson, "The Effects of Two Control Strategies on Children's Emotional Reactions to a Frightening Movie Scene," *Journal of Broadcasting & Electronic Media* 33, no. 4 (1989), https://doi.org/10.1080/08838158909364091.

31. Joanne Cantor and Barbara J. Wilson, "Helping Children Cope with Frightening Media Presentations," *Current Psychology* 7, no. 1 (1988), https://doi.org/10.1007/BF02686664.

32. Cantor, *Mommy, I'm Scared*, 146.

Chapter 8

1. Adam Loewenstein, *Shocking Representation: Historical Trauma, National Cinema, and the Modern Horror Film* (New York: Columbia University Press, 2005).

2. King, *Danse Macabre*.

3. Masahiro Mori, "The Uncanny Valley," in *The Monster Theory Reader*, ed. Jeffrey Andrew Weinstock (Minneapolis: University of Minnesota Press, 2020), 89–94.

4. Maya B. Mathur and David B. Reichling, "Navigating a Social World with Robot Partners: A Quantitative Cartography of the Uncanny Valley," *Cognition* 146 (2016), https://doi.org/10.1016/j.cognition.2015.09.008.

5. Shawn A. Steckenfinger and Asif A. Ghazanfar, "Monkey Visual Behavior Falls into the Uncanny Valley," *Proceedings of the National Academy of Sciences* 106, no. 43 (2009), https://doi.org/10.1073/pnas.0910063106.

6. Mark Schaller and Justin H. Park, "The Behavioral Immune System (and Why It Matters)," *Current Directions in Psychological Science* 20, no. 2 (2011), https://doi.org/10.1177/0963721411402596.

7. Joan M. Sinnott et al., "Perception of Scary Halloween Masks by Zoo Animals and Humans," *International Journal of Comparative Psychology* 25, no. 2 (2012).

8. Joseph E. LeDoux, *The Emotional Brain: The Mysterious Underpinnings of Emotional Life* (New York: Simon & Schuster, 1996).

9. Mark Kermode, *The Exorcist*, 2nd ed. (London: BFI Publishing, 2003), 9.

10. Kermode, *The Exorcist*, 9–10.

11. Jason Zinoman, "Jordan Peele on a Truly Terrifying Monster: Racism," *New York Times*, February 16, 2017, https://www.nytimes.com/2017/02/16/movies/jordan-peele-interview-get-out.html.

12. Brian B. Boutwell, Mathias Clasen, and Jens Kjeldgaard-Christiansen, "'We Are Legion': Possession Myth as a Lens for Understanding Cultural and Psychological Evolution," *Evolutionary Behavioral Sciences* 15, no. 1 (2020): 1–9, https://doi.org/10.1037/ebs0000197.

13. Leeder, *Horror Film*, 87.

14. "100 Years of Horror Movies: IMDb Frequency & Rating," 2018, accessed August 2, 2020, https://imgur.com/a/eZBwaat.

15. Vera Dika, "The Stalker Film, 1978–81," in *American Horrors: Essays on the Modern American Horror Film*, ed. Gregory A. Waller (Chicago: University of Illinois Press, 1987), 86–101.

16. Ménard, Weaver, and Cabrera, "There Are Certain Rules."

17. Zinoman, *Shock Value*.

18. Todd K. Platts, "The New Horror Movie," in *Baby Boomers and Popular Culture: An Inquiry into America's Most Powerful Generation*, ed. Thom Gencarelli and Brian Cogan (Santa Barbara, CA: ABC-Clio, 2014), 147–63.

19. ,"Horror Cinematography: How *Halloween* Scares Audiences," *American Cinematographer*, 2013, accessed February 6, 2021, https://ascmag.com/videos/lighting-tech-tips-household-lightbulb-russell-carpenter-asc-1/horror-cinematography-how-halloween-scares-audiences.

20. James Kendrick, "Slasher Films and Gore in the 1980s," in Benshoff, *Companion to the Horror Film*, 310–28.

21. Craig Ian Mann, "Death and Dead-End Jobs: Independent American Horror and the Great Recession," in *Popular Culture and the Austerity Myth: Hard Times Today*, ed. Pete Bennett and Julian McDougall (Abingdon: Routledge, 2016), 175–88.

22. Scrivner, "Infectious Curiosity."

23. Mathias Clasen, "Imagining the End of the World: A Biocultural Analysis of Post-apocalyptic Fiction," in *Evolution and Popular Narrative*, ed. Dirk Vanderbeke and Brett Cooke (Leiden: Brill, 2019), 64–82.

24. Scrivner et al., "Pandemic Practice."

Chapter 9

1. Clasen, Kjeldgaard-Christiansen, and Johnson, "Horror, Personality."
2. Louise C. Hawkley and John T. Cacioppo, "Loneliness Matters: A Theoretical and Empirical Review of Consequences and Mechanisms," *Annals of Behavioral Medicine* 40, no. 2 (2010), https://doi.org/10.1007/s12160-010-9210-8.
3. Beatrice de Gelder et al., "Fear Fosters Flight: A Mechanism for Fear Contagion When Perceiving Emotion Expressed by a Whole Body," *Proceedings of the National Academy of Sciences of the United States of America* 101, no. 47 (2004), https://doi.org/10.1073/pnas.0407042101.
4. Andreas M. Baranowski, Rebecca Teichmann, and Heiko Hecht, "Canned Emotions. Effects of Genre and Audience Reaction on Emotions," *Art and Perception* 5, no. 3 (2017), https://doi.org/10.1163/22134913-00002068.
5. Erica J. Boothby, Margaret S. Clark, and John A. Bargh, "Shared Experiences Are Amplified," *Psychological Science* 25, no. 12 (2014), https://doi.org/10.1177/0956797614551162.
6. Hanich, *Cinematic Emotion.*
7. Valentijn T. Visch, Ed S. Tan, and Dylan Molenaar, "The Emotional and Cognitive Effect of Immersion in Film Viewing," *Cognition & Emotion* 24, no. 8 (2010), https://doi.org/10.1080/02699930903498186.
8. Neil Lerner, ed., *Music in the Horror Film: Listening to Fear* (New York: Routledge, 2010).
9. Jesse Prinz and Angelika Seidel, "Alligator or Squirrel: Musically Induced Fear Reveals Threat in Ambiguous Figures," *Perception* 41, no. 12 (2012), https://doi.org/10.1068/p7290.
10. Blumstein, Davitian, and Kaye, "Film Soundtracks."
11. K. J. Donnelly, "Hearing Deep Seated Fears: John Carpenter's *The Fog* (1980)," in Lerner, *Music in the Horror Film.*
12. Neil Lerner, "Listening to Fear/Listening with Fear," in Lerner, *Music in the Horror Film.*
13. Sbravatti, "Acoustic Startles."
14. Natalie Zarrelli, "How the Hidden Sounds of Horror Movie Soundtracks Freak You Out," *Atlas Obscura*, October 31, 2016, https://www.atlasobscura.com/articles/how-the-hidden-sounds-of-horror-movie-soundtracks-freak-you-out.
15. Personal communication, July 14, 2020.
16. James H. Geer and Eileen Maisel, "Evaluating the Effects of the Prediction-Control Confound," *Journal of Personality and Social Psychology* 23, no. 3 (1972), https://doi.org/10.1037/h0033122.
17. Andersen et al., "Playing with Fear."
18. Yadan Li et al., "Night or Darkness, Which Intensifies the Feeling of Fear?," *International Journal of Psychophysiology* 97, no. 1 (2015), https://doi.org/10.1016/j.ijpsycho.2015.04.021.

19. Yoo et al., "Human Emotional Brain."

20. Nina N. Rodriguez and Aaron W. Lukaszewski, "Functional Coordination of Personality Strategies with Physical Strength and Attractiveness: A Multi-Sample Investigation at the HEXACO Facet-Level," *Journal of Research in Personality* 89 (2020), https://doi.org/10.1016/j.jrp.2020.104040.

21. John P. Powers and Kevin S. LaBar, "Regulating Emotion through Distancing: A Taxonomy, Neurocognitive Model, and Supporting Meta-Analysis," *Neuroscience & Biobehavioral Reviews* 96 (2019), https://doi.org/10.1016/j.neubiorev.2018.04.023.

22. Yaacov Trope and Nira Liberman, "Construal-Level Theory of Psychological Distance," *Psychological Review* 117, no. 2 (2010), https://doi.org/10.1037/a0018963.

23. Kimberly A. Neuendorf and Glenn G. Sparks, "Predicting Emotional Responses to Horror Films from Cue-Specific Affect," *Communication Quarterly* 36, no. 1 (1988), https://doi.org/10.1080/01463378809369704.

24. Winfried Menninghaus et al., "The Distancing-Embracing Model of the Enjoyment of Negative Emotions in Art Reception," *Behavioral and Brain Sciences* 40 (2017), https://doi.org/10.1017/s0140525x17000309.

25. Green, Brock, and Kaufman, "Understanding Media Enjoyment."

26. Clasen, Andersen, and Schjoedt, "Adrenaline Junkies."

27. Eduardo B. Andrade and Joel B. Cohen, "On the Consumption of Negative Feelings," *Journal of Consumer Research* 34, no. 3 (2007), https://doi.org/10.1086/519498.

28. Gernot Gerger, Helmut Leder, and Alexandra Kremer, "Context Effects on Emotional and Aesthetic Evaluations of Artworks and IAPS Pictures," *Acta Psychologica* 151 (2014), https://doi.org/10.1016/j.actpsy.2014.06.008.

29. Jim Davies, *Imagination: The Science of Your Mind's Greatest Power* (New York: Pegasus, 2019), 43.

30. H. Vaughan Bell et al., "Can Playing the Computer Game 'Tetris' Reduce the Build-Up of Flashbacks for Trauma? A Proposal from Cognitive Science," *PLoS ONE* 4, no. 1 (2009), https://doi.org/10.1371/journal.pone.0004153.

31. Laura Busia and Matteo Griggio, "The Dawn of Social Bonds: What Is the Role of Shared Experiences in Non-Human Animals?," *Biology Letters* 16, no. 7 (2020), https://doi.org/10.1098/rsbl.2020.0201.

32. Brett Cohen, Gordon Waugh, and Karen Place, "At the Movies: An Unobtrusive Study of Arousal-Attraction," *Journal of Social Psychology* 129, no. 5 (1989), https://doi.org/10.1080/00224545.1989.9713786.

References

"65-Yr-Old Dies While Watching Horror Movie." *Times of India* (Chennai), June 17, 2016. https://timesofindia.indiatimes.com/city/chennai/65-yr-old-dies-while-watching-horror-movie/articleshow/52792653.cms.

"100 Years of Horror Movies: IMDb Frequency & Rating." 2018, accessed August 2, 2020. https://imgur.com/a/eZBwaat.

Al-Shawaf, Laith, David M. G. Lewis, and David M. Buss. "Sex Differences in Disgust: Why Are Women More Easily Disgusted Than Men?" *Emotion Review* 10, no. 2 (2017): 149–60. https://doi.org/10.1177/1754073917709940.

Alain, Claude, James Bigelow, and Amy Poremba. "Achilles' Ear? Inferior Human Short-Term and Recognition Memory in the Auditory Modality." *PLoS ONE* 9, no. 2 (2014). https://doi.org/10.1371/journal.pone.0089914.

Aldana Reyes, Xavier. *Horror Film and Affect: Towards a Corporeal Model of Viewership.* New York: Routledge, 2016.

Almeida, Alishya. "*Parasite* as Horror Film." *Horror Homeroom*, July 7, 2020. http://www.horrorhomeroom.com/parasite-as-horror-film/.

Andersen, Marc Malmdorf, Uffe Schjoedt, Henry Price, Fernando Rosas, Coltan Scrivner, and Mathias Clasen. "Playing with Fear: A Field Study in Recreational Horror." *Psychological Science* 31, no. 12 (2020): 1497–512. https://doi.org/10.1177/0956797620972116.

Andrade, Eduardo B., and Joel B. Cohen. "On the Consumption of Negative Feelings." *Journal of Consumer Research* 34, no. 3 (2007): 283–300. https://doi.org/10.1086/519498.

Andrews, David. "The Rape-Revenge Film: Biocultural Implications." *Jump Cut: A Review of Contemporary Media*, no. 54. (2012). http://www.ejumpcut.org/archive/jc54.2012/DAndrewsRapeRevenge/.

"Annabelle Reviews—Metacritic." *Metacritic*, accessed August 2, 2020. https://www.metacritic.com/movie/annabelle.

Antunes, Filipa. *Children Beware! Childhood, Horror and the PG-13 Rating.* Jefferson, NC: McFarland, 2020.

Aristotle. *Poetics.* Translated by Malcolm Heath. New York: Penguin, 1997.

Arnzen, Michael A. "Who's Laughing Now? The Postmodern Splatter Film." *Journal of Popular Film and Television* 21, no. 4 (1994): 176–84. https://doi.org/10.1080/01956051.1994.9943985.

Baird, Robert. "The Startle Effect: Implications for Spectator Cognition and Media Theory." *Film Quarterly* 53, no. 3 (2000): 12–24. https://doi.org/10.1525/fq.2000.53.3.04a00030.

Ballon, Bruce, and Molyn Leszcz. "Horror Films: Tales to Master Terror or Shapers of Trauma?" *American Journal of Psychotherapy* 61, no. 2 (2007): 211–30. https://doi.org/10.1176/appi.psychotherapy.2007.61.2.211.

Baranowski, Andreas M., Rebecca Teichmann, and Heiko Hecht. "Canned Emotions: Effects of Genre and Audience Reaction on Emotions." *Art and Perception* 5, no. 3 (2017): 312–36. https://doi.org/10.1163/22134913-00002068.

Barber, Nicholas. "Is Horror the Most Disrespected Genre?" *BBC Culture*, June 14, 2018. https://www.bbc.com/culture/article/20180614-is-horror-the-most-disrespected-genre.

Barker, Martin. "The UK 'Video Nasties' Campaign Revisited: Panics, Claims-Making, Risks, and Politics." In *Discourses of Anxiety over Childhood and Youth across Cultures*, edited by Liza Tsaliki and Despina Chronaki, 29–50. Cham: Springer, 2020.

Bastian, Brock, Jolanda Jetten, and Laura J. Ferris. "Pain as Social Glue." *Psychological Science* 25, no. 11 (2014): 2079–85. https://doi.org/10.1177/0956797614545886.

Bell, Vaughan, Emily A. Holmes, Ella L. James, Thomas Coode-Bate, and Catherine Deeprose. "Can Playing the Computer Game 'Tetris' Reduce the Build-Up of Flashbacks for Trauma? A Proposal from Cognitive Science." *PLoS ONE* 4, no. 1 (2009). https://doi.org/10.1371/journal.pone.0004153.

Bjorklund, David F., and Anthony D. Pellegrini. *The Origins of Human Nature: Evolutionary Developmental Psychology.* Washington, DC: American Psychological Association, 2002.

Blumstein, Daniel T., Richard Davitian, and Peter D. Kaye. "Do Film Soundtracks Contain Nonlinear Analogues to Influence Emotion?" *Biology Letters* 6, no. 6 (2010): 751–54. https://doi.org/10.1098/rsbl.2010.0333.

Bologna, Caroline. "Why Some People with Anxiety Love Watching Horror Movies." *Huffington Post*, October 31, 2019. https://www.huffpost.com/entry/anxiety-love-watching-horror-movies_l_5d277587e4b02a5a5d57b59e.

Bonin, Patrick, Gaëtan Thiebaut, Pavol Prokop, and Alain Méot. "'In Your Head, Zombie': Zombies, Predation and Memory." *Journal of Cognitive Psychology* 31, no. 7 (2019): 635–50. https://doi.org/10.1080/20445911.2019.1664557.

Boothby, Erica J., Margaret S. Clark, and John A. Bargh. "Shared Experiences Are Amplified." *Psychological Science* 25, no. 12 (2014): 2209–16. https://doi.org/10.1177/0956797614551162.

Boutwell, Brian B., Mathias Clasen, and Jens Kjeldgaard-Christiansen. "'We Are Legion': Possession Myth as a Lens for Understanding Cultural and Psychological Evolution." *Evolutionary Behavioral Sciences* 15, no. 1 (2020): 1–9. https://doi.org/10.1037/ebs0000197.

Boyer, Pascal, and Brian Bergstrom. "Threat-Detection in Child Development: An Evolutionary Perspective." *Neuroscience & Biobehavioral Reviews* 35, no. 4 (2011): 1034–41. https://doi.org/10.1016/j.neubiorev.2010.08.010.

Bozzuto, James C. "Cinematic Neurosis Following 'The Exorcist': Report of Four Cases." *Journal of Nervous and Mental Disease* 161, no. 1 (1975): 43–48. https://doi.org/10.1097/00005053-197507000-00005.

Buckingham, David. *Moving Images: Understanding Children's Emotional Responses to Television*. Manchester: Manchester University Press, 1996.

Busia, Laura, and Matteo Griggio. "The Dawn of Social Bonds: What Is the Role of Shared Experiences in Non-Human Animals?" *Biology Letters* 16, no. 7 (2020). https://doi.org/10.1098/rsbl.2020.0201.

Buss, David M., ed. *The Handbook of Evolutionary Psychology*. 2nd ed. Hoboken, NJ: John Wiley & Sons, 2016.

Campbell, Anne. "Survival, Selection, and Sex Differences in Fear." In *The Cambridge Handbook of Evolutionary Perspectives on Human Behavior*, edited by Lance Workman, Will Reader, and Jerome H. Barkow, 313–29. Cambridge: Cambridge University Press, 2020.

Cannon, Walter B. *Bodily Changes in Pain, Hunger, Fear and Rage: An Account of Recent Researches into the Function of Emotional Excitement*. New York: D. Appleton, 1915. doi:10.1037/10013-000.

Cannon, Walter B. "'Voodoo' Death." *American Anthropologist* 44, no. 2 (1942): 169–81. https://doi.org/10.1525/aa.1942.44.2.02a00010.

Cantor, Joanne. "Fright Reactions to Mass Media." In *Media Effects: Advances in Theory and Research*, edited by Jennings Bryant and Mary Beth Oliver, 287–303. New York: Routledge, 2009.

Cantor, Joanne. "'I'll Never Have a Clown in My House'—Why Movie Horror Lives On." *Poetics Today* 25, no. 2 (2004): 283–304. http://muse.jhu.edu/journals/poetics_today/v025/25.2cantor.html.

Cantor, Joanne. *"Mommy, I'm Scared": How TV and Movies Frighten Children and What We Can Do to Protect Them*. Orlando, FL: Harcourt Brace, 1998.

Cantor, Joanne, and Mary Beth Oliver. "Developmental Differences in Responses to Horror." In *Horror Films: Research on Audience Preference and Reactions*, edited by J. B. Weaver and R. Tamborini, 63–80. Hillsdale, NJ: Lawrence Erlbaum, 1996.

Cantor, Joanne, and Barbara J. Wilson. "Helping Children Cope with Frightening Media Presentations." *Current Psychology* 7, no. 1 (1988): 58–75. https://doi.org/10.1007/BF02686664.

Cantor, Joanne, and Barbara J. Wilson. "Modifying Fear Responses to Mass Media in Preschool and Elementary School Children." *Journal of Broadcasting* 28, no. 4 (2009): 431–43. https://doi.org/10.1080/08838158409386552.

Carleton, R. Nicholas. "Fear of the Unknown: One Fear to Rule Them All?" *Journal of Anxiety Disorders* 41 (2016): 5–21. https://doi.org/http://dx.doi.org/10.1016/j.janxdis.2016.03.011.

Carroll, Joseph. "Death in Literature." In *Evolutionary Perspectives on Death*, edited by Todd K. Shackelford and Virgil Zeigler-Hill, 137–59. New York: Springer, 2019.

Carroll, Joseph. "Imagination, the Brain's Default Mode Network, and Imaginative Verbal Artifacts." In *Evolutionary Perspectives on Imaginative Culture*, edited by Joseph Carroll, Mathias Clasen, and Emelie Jonsson, 31–52. New York: Springer, 2020.

Carroll, Joseph, Jonathan Gottschall, John A. Johnson, and Daniel J. Kruger. *Graphing Jane Austen: The Evolutionary Basis of Literary Meaning*. Basingstoke: Palgrave Macmillan, 2012.

Choi, Jinhee. "Fits and Startles: Cognitivism Revisited." *Journal of Aesthetics and Art Criticism* 61, no. 2 (2003): 149–57. https://doi.org/10.1111/1540-6245.00102.

Clark, Christina, and Amelia Foster. *Children's and Young People's Reading Habits and Preferences: The Who, What, Why, Where and When.* London: National Literacy Trust, 2005. https://files.eric.ed.gov/fulltext/ED541603.pdf.

Clasen, Mathias. "Hauntings of Human Nature: An Evolutionary Critique of King's *The Shining.*" *Style* 51, no. 1 (2017): 76–88.

Clasen, Mathias. "Imagining the End of the World: A Biocultural Analysis of Post-Apocalyptic Fiction." In *Evolution and Popular Narrative*, edited by Dirk Vanderbeke and Brett Cooke, 64–82. Leiden: Brill, 2019.

Clasen, Mathias. *Why Horror Seduces.* New York: Oxford University Press, 2017.

Clasen, Mathias, Marc Andersen, and Uffe Schjoedt. "Adrenaline Junkies and White-Knucklers: A Quantitative Study of Fear Management in Haunted House Visitors." *Poetics* 73 (2019): 61–71. https://doi.org/10.1016/j.poetic.2019.01.002.

Clasen, Mathias, Jens Kjeldgaard-Christiansen, and John A. Johnson. "Horror, Personality, and Threat Simulation: A Survey on the Psychology of Scary Media." *Evolutionary Behavioral Sciences* 14, no. 3 (2020): 213–30. https://doi.org/10.1037/ebs0000152.

Clepper, Catherine. "'Death by Fright': Risk, Consent, and Evidentiary Objects in William Castle's Rigged Houses." *Film History* 28, no. 3 (2016): 54–84. https://doi.org/10.2979/filmhistory.28.3.04.

Cochrane, Kira. "For Your Entertainment." *The Guardian* (London), May 1, 2007. https://www.theguardian.com/film/2007/may/01/gender.world.

Cohen, Brett, Gordon Waugh, and Karen Place. "At the Movies: An Unobtrusive Study of Arousal-Attraction." *Journal of Social Psychology* 129, no. 5 (1989): 691–93. https://doi.org/10.1080/00224545.1989.9713786.

Cools, Joseph, David E. Schotte, and Richard J. McNally. "Emotional Arousal and Overeating in Restrained Eaters." *Journal of Abnormal Psychology* 101, no. 2 (1992): 348–51. https://doi.org/10.1037/0021-843x.101.2.348.

Crucchiola, Jordan. "What Makes the New Horror Film *It Follows* So Damn Good." *Wired*, March 17, 2015. https://www.wired.com/2015/03/it-follows-unholy-trinity/.

Cundey, Dean. "Horror Cinematography: How *Halloween* Scares Audiences." *American Cinematographer*, 2013, accessed February 6, 2021. https://ascmag.com/videos/lighting-tech-tips-household-lightbulb-russell-carpenter-asc-1/horror-cinematography-how-halloween-scares-audiences.

Curtis, Val, Robert Aunger, and Tamer Rabie. "Evidence That Disgust Evolved to Protect from Risk of Disease." *Proceedings of the Royal Society of London B: Biological Sciences* 271, Suppl 4 (2004): S131–S33. https://doi.org/10.1098/rsbl.2003.0144.

Dahl, Gordon, and Stefano DellaVigna. "Does Movie Violence Increase Violent Crime?" *Quarterly Journal of Economics* 124, no. 2 (2009): 677–734. https://doi.org/10.1162/qjec.2009.124.2.677.

Daniels, Les. *Living in Fear: A History of Horror in the Mass Media.* New York: Da Capo Press, 1975.

Davies, Jim. *Imagination: The Science of Your Mind's Greatest Power.* New York: Pegasus, 2019.

Davis, Blair, and Kial Natale. "'The Pound of Flesh Which I Demand.'" In *American Horror Film: The Genre at the Turn of the Millennium*, edited by Steffen Hantke, 35–56. Jackson: University Press of Mississippi, 2010.

de Gelder, Beatrice, Josh Snyder, Doug Greve, George Gerard, and Nouchine Hadjikhani. "Fear Fosters Flight: A Mechanism for Fear Contagion When Perceiving Emotion Expressed by a Whole Body." *Proceedings of the National Academy of Sciences of the United States of America* 101, no. 47 (2004): 16701–6. https://doi.org/10.1073/pnas.0407042101.

del Toro, Guillermo. "Haunted Castles, Dark Mirrors: On the Penguin Horror Series." In *The Thing on the Doorstep and Other Weird Stories*, edited by S. T. Joshi, 1–14. New York: Penguin, 2013.

Dika, Vera. "The Stalker Film, 1978-81." In *American Horrors: Essays on the Modern American Horror Film*, edited by Gregory A. Waller, 86–101. Urbana: University of Illinois Press, 1987.

"Do Modern Horror Movies Contain More Jump Scares Than Older Movies?" HacShac, 2020, accessed July 24, 2020. https://wheresthejump.com/do-modern-horror-movies-contain-more-jump-scares-than-older-movies/.

Donnelly, K. J. "Hearing Deep Seated Fears: John Carpenter's *The Fog* (1980)." In *Music in the Horror Film: Listening to Fear*, edited by Neil Lerner, 152–67. New York: Routledge, 2010.

Dutton, Denis. *The Art Instinct: Beauty, Pleasure, & Human Evolution.* New York: Bloomsbury Press, 2009.

Dutton, Donald G., and Arthur P. Aron. "Some Evidence for Heightened Sexual Attraction under Conditions of High Anxiety." *Journal of Personality and Social Psychology* 30, no. 4 (1974): 510–17. https://doi.org/10.1037/h0037031.

Ebert, Roger. "The Exorcist." *Chicago Sun-Times*, December 26, 1973. https://www.rogerebert.com/reviews/the-exorcist-1973.

Edelstein, David. "Now Playing at Your Local Multiplex: Torture Porn." *New York Magazine*, January 26, 2006. https://nymag.com/movies/features/15622/.

Eden, Allison, Mary Beth Oliver, Ron Tamborini, Anthony Limperos, and Julia Woolley. "Perceptions of Moral Violations and Personality Traits among Heroes and Villains." *Mass Communication and Society* 18, no. 2 (2014): 186–208. https://doi.org/10.1080/15205436.2014.923462.

"Eli Roth Talks Hostel: Part II, the Internet, the MPAA and More." *Movieweb*, 2007, accessed August 2, 2020. https://movieweb.com/eli-roth-talks-hostel-part-ii-the-internet-the-mpaa-and-more/.

"The Exorcist." *Variety*, December 31, 1973. https://variety.com/1972/film/reviews/the-exorcist-2-1200422937/.

"Exorcist Fever." *Time*, February 11, 1974, 53.

Ferguson, Christopher J. *Adolescents, Crime, and the Media: A Critical Analysis.* New York: Springer, 2013.

Ferguson, Christopher J. "Does Media Violence Predict Societal Violence? It Depends on What You Look at and When." *Journal of Communication* 65, no. 1 (2015): E1–E22. https://doi.org/10.1111/jcom.12129.

Follows, Stephen. *The Horror Report*. n.p.: Film Data Fund, 2017.

Frijda, Nico H. *The Emotions*. Cambridge: Cambridge University Press, 1986.

Garris, Mick. *Post Mortem with Mick Garris*. Podcast audio. 57: Joe Dante—Live from the 2019 Lucca Film Festival, 2019. https://www.stitcher.com/podcast/blumhouse/post-mortem-with-mick-garris/e/62018160.

Garris, Mick. *Post Mortem with Mick Garris*. Podcast audio. 90: Guillermo del Toro, 2020. https://www.stitcher.com/podcast/blumhouse/post-mortem-with-mick-garris/e/69782024.

Geer, James H., and Eileen Maisel. "Evaluating the Effects of the Prediction-Control Confound." *Journal of Personality and Social Psychology* 23, no. 3 (1972): 314–19. https://doi.org/10.1037/h0033122.

Gerger, Gernot, Helmut Leder, and Alexandra Kremer. "Context Effects on Emotional and Aesthetic Evaluations of Artworks and IAPS Pictures." *Acta Psychologica* 151 (2014): 174–83. https://doi.org/10.1016/j.actpsy.2014.06.008.

Götz, Maya, Dafna Lemish, and Andrea Holler. *Fear in Front of the Screen: Children's Fears, Nightmares, and Thrills from TV*. Lanham, MD: Rowman & Littlefield, 2019.

Green, Melanie C., Timothy C. Brock, and Geoff F. Kaufman. "Understanding Media Enjoyment: The Role of Transportation into Narrative Worlds." *Communication Theory* 14, no. 4 (2004): 311–27. https://doi.org/10.1111/j.1468-2885.2004.tb00317.x.

Grillon, Christian, Rezvan Ameli, Scott W. Woods, Kathleen Merikangas, and Michael Davis. "Fear-Potentiated Startle in Humans: Effects of Anticipatory Anxiety on the Acoustic Blink Reflex." *Psychophysiology* 28, no. 5 (1991): 588–95. https://doi.org/10.1111/j.1469-8986.1991.tb01999.x.

Grillon, Christian, and Michael Davis. "Fear-Potentiated Startle Conditioning in Humans: Explicit and Contextual Cue Conditioning Following Paired versus Unpaired Training." *Psychophysiology* 34, no. 4 (1997): 451–58. http://www.ncbi.nlm.nih.gov/pubmed/9260498.

Grillon, Christian, David Quispe-Escudero, Ambika Mathur, and Monique Ernst. "Mental Fatigue Impairs Emotion Regulation." *Emotion* 15, no. 3 (2015): 383–89. https://doi.org/10.1037/emo0000058.

Hajdu, David. *The Ten-Cent Plague: The Great Comic-Book Scare and How It Changed America*. New York: Farrar, Straus and Giroux, 2008.

Hanich, Julian. *Cinematic Emotion in Horror Films and Thrillers: The Aesthetic Paradox of Pleasurable Fear*. New York: Routledge, 2010.

Hantke, Steffen. "'They Don't Make 'Em Like They Used To': On the Rhetoric of Crisis and the Current State of American Horror Cinema." In *American Horror Film: The Genre at the Turn of the Millennium*, edited by Steffen Hantke, vi–xiv. Jackson: University Press of Mississippi, 2010.

Harris, Paul L., Emma Brown, Crispin Marriott, Samantha Whittall, and Sarah Harmer. "Monsters, Ghosts and Witches: Testing the Limits of the Fantasy-Reality

Distinction in Young Children." *British Journal of Developmental Psychology* 9, no. 1 (1991): 105–23. https://doi.org/10.1111/j.2044-835X.1991.tb00865.x.

Harris, Richard Jackson, Steven J. Hoekstra, Christina L. Scott, Fred W. Sanborn, Joseph Andrew Karafa, and Jason Dean Brandenburg. "Young Men's and Women's Different Autobiographical Memories of the Experience of Seeing Frightening Movies on a Date." *Media Psychology* 2, no. 3 (2000): 245–68. https://doi.org/10.1207/s1532785xmep0203_3.

Harrison, Kristen, and Joanne Cantor. "Tales from the Screen: Enduring Fright Reactions to Scary Media." *Media Psychology* 1, no. 2 (1999): 97–116. https://doi.org/10.1207/s1532785xmep0102_1.

Hawkley, Louise C., and John T. Cacioppo. "Loneliness Matters: A Theoretical and Empirical Review of Consequences and Mechanisms." *Annals of Behavioral Medicine* 40, no. 2 (2010): 218–27. https://doi.org/10.1007/s12160-010-9210-8.

Hayes, Britt. "'Hereditary' Director Ari Aster on Why He Avoided Calling His Terrifying Debut a 'Horror Film.'" *ScreenCrush*, June 7, 2018. https://screencrush.com/ari-aster-interview-hereditary/.

Hoekstra, Steven J., Richard Jackson Harris, and Angela L. Helmick. "Autobiographical Memories about the Experience of Seeing Frightening Movies in Childhood." *Media Psychology* 1, no. 2 (1999): 117–40. https://doi.org/10.1207/s1532785xmep0102_2.

Hoffner, Cynthia A., and Joanne Cantor. "Developmental Differences in Responses to a Television Character's Appearance and Behavior." *Developmental Psychology* 21, no. 6 (1985): 1065–74. https://doi.org/10.1037/0012-1649.21.6.1065.

Hoffner, Cynthia A., and Kenneth J. Levine. "Enjoyment of Mediated Fright and Violence: A Meta-Analysis." *Media Psychology* 7, no. 2 (2005): 207–37. https://doi.org/10.1207/S1532785XMEP0702_5.

Hudson, Matthew, Kerttu Seppälä, Vesa Putkinen, Lihua Sun, Enrico Glerean, Tomi Karjalainen, Henry K. Karlsson, Jussi Hirvonen, and Lauri Nummenmaa. "Dissociable Neural Systems for Unconditioned Acute and Sustained Fear." *NeuroImage* 216 (2020). https://doi.org/10.1016/j.neuroimage.2020.116522.

Hye-Knudsen, Marc, and Mathias Clasen. "'So-Bad-It's-Good': *The Room* and the Paradoxical Appeal of Bad Films." *16:9*, November 28, 2019. http://www.16-9.dk/2019/11/so-bad-its-good/.

Izard, Carroll E. *Human Emotions.* New York: Plenum Press, 1977.

Jancovich, Mark. "Genre and the Audience: Genre Classifications and Cultural Distinctions in the Mediation of *The Silence of the Lambs*." In *Horror, the Film Reader*, edited by Mark Jancovich, 151–61. London: Routledge, 2002.

Jones, Steve. *Torture Porn: Popular Horror after Saw.* London: Palgrave Macmillan, 2013.

Kazanas, Stephanie A., and Jeanette Altarriba. "Did Our Ancestors Fear the Unknown? The Role of Predation in the Survival Advantage." *Evolutionary Behavioral Sciences* 11, no. 1 (2017): 83–91. https://doi.org/10.1037/ebs0000074.

Kendrick, James. "Slasher Films and Gore in the 1980s." In *A Companion to the Horror Film*, edited by Harry M. Benshoff, 310–28. Malden, MA: John Wiley & Sons, 2014.

Kermode, Mark. *The Exorcist*. Rev. ed. London: BFI Publishing, 2003.

Kerner, Aaron. *Torture Porn in the Wake of 9/11: Horror, Exploitation, and the Cinema of Sensation*. New Brunswick, NJ: Rutgers University Press, 2015.

Kerr, Margee, Greg J. Siegle, and Jahala Orsini. "Voluntary Arousing Negative Experiences (VANE): Why We Like to Be Scared." *Emotion* 19, no. 4 (2019): 682–98. https://doi.org/10.1037/emo0000470.

King, Stephen. *Danse Macabre*. New York: Berkley Books, 1983.

King, Stephen. *'Salem's Lot*. London: Hodder & Stoughton, 2008.

King, Wayne. "Nightmares Suspected in Bed Deaths of 18 Laotians." *New York Times*, May 10, 1981, 21. https://www.nytimes.com/1981/05/10/us/nightmares-suspected-in-bed-deaths-of-18-laotians.html.

Kirby, Terry. "Video Link to Bulger Murder Disputed." *The Independent* (London), November 26, 1993. https://www.independent.co.uk/news/video-link-to-bulger-murder-disputed-1506766.html.

Kjeldgaard-Christiansen, Jens. "A Structure of Antipathy: Constructing the Villain in Narrative Film." *Projections* 13, no. 1 (2019): 67–90. https://doi.org/10.3167/proj.2019.130105.

Kjeldgaard-Christiansen, Jens, and Sarah Helene Schmidt. "Disney's Shifting Visions of Villainy from the 1990s to the 2010s: A Biocultural Analysis." *Evolutionary Studies in Imaginative Culture* 3, no. 2 (2019): 1–16. https://doi.org/10.26613/esic.3.2.140.

Klemesrud, Judy. "They Wait Hours—to Be Shocked." *New York Times*, January 27, 1974. https://www.nytimes.com/1974/01/27/archives/they-wait-hoursto-be-shocked-the-exorcist-got-mixed-reviews-why-has.html.

Kruuk, Hans. *Hunter and Hunted: Relationships between Carnivores and People*. Cambridge: Cambridge University Press, 2002.

Lang, Peter J., Margaret M. Bradley, and Bruce N. Cuthbert. "Emotion, Attention, and the Startle Reflex." *Psychological Review* 97, no. 3 (1990): 377–95. https://doi.org/10.1037/0033-295x.97.3.377.

Lanska, Douglas J. "Jumping Frenchmen, Miryachit, and Latah: Culture-Specific Hyperstartle-Plus Syndromes." *Frontiers of Neurology and Neuroscience* 42 (2018): 122–31. https://doi.org/ 10.1159/000475700.

LeDoux, Joseph E. *The Emotional Brain: The Mysterious Underpinnings of Emotional Life*. New York: Simon & Schuster, 1996.

Leeder, Murray. *Horror Film: A Critical Introduction*. New York: Bloomsbury Academic, 2018.

Lerner, Neil. "Listening to Fear / Listening with Fear." In *Music in the Horror Film: Listening to Fear*, edited by Neil Lerner, viii–xi. New York: Routledge, 2010.

Lerner, Neil, ed. *Music in the Horror Film: Listening to Fear*. New York: Routledge, 2010.

Lester, Catherine. "The Children's Horror Film: Characterizing an 'Impossible' Subgenre." *Velvet Light Trap* 78 (2016): 22–37. https://doi.org/10.7560/vlt7803.

Li, Yadan, Wenjuan Ma, Qin Kang, Lei Qiao, Dandan Tang, Jiang Qiu, Qinglin Zhang, and Hong Li. "Night or Darkness, Which Intensifies the Feeling of Fear?" *International Journal of Psychophysiology* 97, no. 1 (2015): 46–57. https://doi.org/10.1016/j.ijpsycho.2015.04.021.

Loewenstein, Adam. *Shocking Representation: Historical Trauma, National Cinema, and the Modern Horror Film*. New York: Columbia University Press, 2005.

Mann, Craig Ian. "Death and Dead-End Jobs: Independent American Horror and the Great Recession." In *Popular Culture and the Austerity Myth: Hard Times Today*, edited by Pete Bennett and Julian McDougall, 175–88. Abingdon: Routledge, 2016.

Manson, Frederick. "Notes of a Case of Death from Fright." *The Lancet* 48, no. 1213 (1846). https://doi.org/10.1016/s0140-6736(02)89361-8.

Mar, Raymond A., and Keith Oatley. "The Function of Fiction Is the Abstraction and Simulation of Social Experience." *Perspectives on Psychological Science* 3, no. 3 (2008): 173–92. https://doi.org/10.1111/j.1745-6924.2008.00073.x.

Markey, Patrick M., Juliana E. French, and Charlotte N. Markey. "Violent Movies and Severe Acts of Violence: Sensationalism versus Science." *Human Communication Research* 41, no. 2 (2015): 155–73. https://doi.org/10.1111/hcre.12046.

Marks, Craig, and Rob Tannenbaum. "Freddy Lives: An Oral History of *A Nightmare on Elm Street*." *Vulture*, October 20, 2014. https://www.vulture.com/2014/10/nightmare-on-elm-street-oral-history.html.

Martin, G. Neil. "(Why) Do You Like Scary Movies? A Review of the Empirical Research on Psychological Responses to Horror Films." *Frontiers in Psychology* 10 (2019). https://doi.org/10.3389/fpsyg.2019.02298.

Mathur, Maya B., and David B. Reichling. "Navigating a Social World with Robot Partners: A Quantitative Cartography of the Uncanny Valley." *Cognition* 146 (2016): 22–32. https://doi.org/10.1016/j.cognition.2015.09.008.

McGraw, A. Peter, and Caleb Warren. "Benign Violations: Making Immoral Behavior Funny." *Psychological Science* 21, no. 8 (2010): 1141–49. https://doi.org/10.1177/0956797610376073.

Ménard, A. Dana, Angela Weaver, and Christine Cabrera. "'There Are Certain Rules That One Must Abide By': Predictors of Mortality in Slasher Films." *Sexuality & Culture* 23, no. 2 (2019): 621–40. https://doi.org/10.1007/s12119-018-09583-2.

Menninghaus, Winfried, Valentin Wagner, Julian Hanich, Eugen Wassiliwizky, Thomas Jacobsen, and Stefan Koelsch. "The Distancing-Embracing Model of the Enjoyment of Negative Emotions in Art Reception." *Behavioral and Brain Sciences* 40 (2017): e347. https://doi.org/10.1017/s0140525x17000309.

Meza, Ed. "Guillermo del Toro on the Catholic Church, His Holy Trinity and Boris Karloff Epiphany." *Variety*, October 17, 2017. https://variety.com/2017/film/festivals/guillermo-del-toro-masterclass-2017-lumiere-festival-1202591885/.

Mian, Rubina, Graham Shelton-Rayner, Brendan Harkin, and Paul Williams. "Observing a Fictitious Stressful Event: Haematological Changes, Including Circulating Leukocyte Activation." *Stress* 6, no. 1 (2009): 41–47. https://doi.org/10.1080/1025389031000101349.

Mori, Masahiro. "The Uncanny Valley." In *The Monster Theory Reader*, edited by Jeffrey Andrew Weinstock, 89–94. Minneapolis: University of Minnesota Press, 2020.

Moss, Abby. "Why Some Anxious People Find Comfort in Horror Movies." *Vice*, November 8, 2017. https://www.vice.com/en_us/article/a3wdzk/why-some-anxious-people-find-comfort-in-horror-movies.

Mulukom, Valerie van. "The Evolution of Imagination and Fiction through Generativity and Narrative." In *Evolutionary Perspectives on Imaginative Culture*, edited by Joseph Carroll, Mathias Clasen, and Emelie Jonsson, 53–70. New York: Springer, 2020.

Muzio, Gianluca Di. "The Immorality of Horror Films." *International Journal of Applied Philosophy* 20, no. 2 (2006): 277–94. https://doi.org/10.5840/ijap200620222.

Nairne, James S., Sarah R. Thompson, and Josefa N. S. Pandeirada. "Adaptive Memory: Survival Processing Enhances Retention." *Journal of Experimental Psychology: Learning, Memory, and Cognition* 33, no. 2 (2007): 263–73. https://doi.org/10.1037/0278-7393.33.2.263.

Nemeth, Banne, Luuk J. J. Scheres, Willem M. Lijfering, and Frits R. Rosendaal. "Bloodcurdling Movies and Measures of Coagulation: Fear Factor Crossover Trial." *BMJ* (2015): h6367. https://doi.org/10.1136/bmj.h6367.

Nesse, Randolph M. "The Smoke Detector Principle." *Annals of the New York Academy of Sciences* 935, no. 1 (2006): 75–85. https://doi.org/10.1111/j.1749-6632.2001.tb03472.x.

Neuendorf, Kimberly A., and Glenn G. Sparks. "Predicting Emotional Responses to Horror Films from Cue-Specific Affect." *Communication Quarterly* 36, no. 1 (1988): 16–27. https://doi.org/10.1080/01463378809369704.

Newman, Kim. *Nightmare Movies: Horror on Screen since the 1960s*. Rev. ed. London: Bloomsbury Publishing, 2011.

Nicholson, Tom. "The 2010s Were the Decade When Horror Got Smart." *Esquire*, December 20, 2019. https://www.esquire.com/uk/culture/film/a30284121/elevated-horror-2010s-peele-eggers-aster-blumhouse/.

Noble, R. E. "Stephen King Wrist." *Western Journal of Medicine* 171, no. 2 (1999): 80.

Nowell, Richard. *Blood Money: A History of the First Teen Slasher Film Cycle*. New York: Continuum, 2011.

Nowell, Richard. "'There's More Than One Way to Lose Your Heart': The American Film Industry, Early Teen Slasher Films, and Female Youth." *Cinema Journal* 51, no. 1 (2011): 115–40.

Öhman, Arne, and Susan Mineka. "Fears, Phobias, and Preparedness: Toward an Evolved Module of Fear and Fear Learning." *Psychological Review* 108, no. 3 (2001): 483–522. http://www.ncbi.nlm.nih.gov/pubmed/11488376.

Palmer, Edward L., Anne B. Hockett, and Walter W. Dean. "The Television Family and Children's Fright Reactions." *Journal of Family Issues* 4, no. 2 (2016): 279–92. https://doi.org/10.1177/019251383004002002.

Parker, Karen J., Christine L. Buckmaster, Shellie A. Hyde, Alan F. Schatzberg, and David M. Lyons. "Nonlinear Relationship between Early Life Stress Exposure and Subsequent Resilience in Monkeys." *Scientific Reports* 9, no. 1 (2019): 16232. https://doi.org/10.1038/s41598-019-52810-5.

Pascale, Marius A. "Art Horror, Reactive Attitudes, and Compassionate Slashers." *International Journal of Applied Philosophy* 33, no. 1 (2019): 141–59. https://doi.org/10.5840/ijap201981116.

Petley, Julian. "'Are We Insane?' The 'Video Nasty' Moral Panic." *Recherches sociologiques et anthropologiques* 43, no. 1 (2012): 35–57. https://doi.org/10.4000/rsa.839.

Phelan, Laurence. "Film Censorship: How Moral Panic Led to a Mass Ban of 'Video Nasties.'" *The Independent* (London), July 13, 2015. https://www.independent.co.uk/arts-entertainment/films/features/film-censorship-how-moral-panic-led-to-a-mass-ban-of-video-nasties-9600998.html.

Pinedo, Isabel C. "Torture Porn." In *A Companion to the Horror Film*, edited by Harry M. Benshoff, 345–61. Hoboken, NJ: John Wiley & Sons, 2014.

Plantinga, Carl. "The Scene of Empathy and the Human Face on Film." In *Passionate Views: Film, Cognition, and Emotion*, edited by Carl Plantinga and Greg M. Smith, 239–55. Baltimore: Johns Hopkins University Press, 1999.

Platts, Todd K. "The New Horror Movie." In *Baby Boomers and Popular Culture: An Inquiry into America's Most Powerful Generation*, edited by Thom Gencarelli and Brian Cogan, 147–63. Santa Barbara, CA: ABC-Clio, 2014.

Platts, Todd K., and Mathias Clasen. "Scary Business: Horror at the North American Box Office, 2006–2016." *Frames Cinema Journal*, no. 11 (2017). http://framescinemajournal.com/article/scary-business-horror-at-the-north-american-box-office-2006-2016/.

Powers, John P., and Kevin S. LaBar. "Regulating Emotion through Distancing: A Taxonomy, Neurocognitive Model, and Supporting Meta-Analysis." *Neuroscience & Biobehavioral Reviews* 96 (2019): 155–73. https://doi.org/10.1016/j.neubiorev.2018.04.023.

Prinz, Jesse, and Angelika Seidel. "Alligator or Squirrel: Musically Induced Fear Reveals Threat in Ambiguous Figures." *Perception* 41, no. 12 (2012): 1535–39. https://doi.org/10.1068/p7290.

Punter, David. *The Literature of Terror: A History of Gothic Fictions from 1765 to the Present Day*. 2 vols. New York: Longman, 1996.

Ramos, Raul A., Christopher J. Ferguson, Kelly Frailing, and Maria Romero-Ramirez. "Comfortably Numb or Just Yet Another Movie? Media Violence Exposure Does Not Reduce Viewer Empathy for Victims of Real Violence among Primarily Hispanic Viewers." *Psychology of Popular Media Culture* 2, no. 1 (2013): 2–10. https://doi.org/10.1037/a0030119.

"Report of the Media Violence Commission." *Aggressive Behavior* 38, no. 5 (2012): 335–41. https://doi.org/10.1002/ab.21443.

Revonsuo, Antti. "The Reinterpretation of Dreams: An Evolutionary Hypothesis of the Function of Dreaming." *Behavioral and Brain Sciences* 23, no. 6 (2000): 877–901. http://www.ncbi.nlm.nih.gov/pubmed/11515147.

Robinson, Jenefer. "Startle." *Journal of Philosophy* 92, no. 2 (1995): 53–74. https://doi.org/10.2307/2940940.

Robinson, Tom, Clark Callahan, and Keith Evans. "Why Do We Keep Going Back? A Q Method Analysis of Our Attraction to Horror Movies." *Operant Subjectivity* 37, nos. 1–2 (2014): 41–57.

Rodriguez, Nina N., and Aaron W. Lukaszewski. "Functional Coordination of Personality Strategies with Physical Strength and Attractiveness: A Multi-Sample Investigation at the HEXACO Facet-Level." *Journal of Research in Personality* 89 (2020): 104040. https://doi.org/10.1016/j.jrp.2020.104040.

Rose, Steve. "How Post-Horror Movies Are Taking over Cinema." *The Guardian* (London), July 6, 2017. https://www.theguardian.com/film/2017/jul/06/post-horror-films-scary-movies-ghost-story-it-comes-at-night.

Rudder, Christian. "The Best Questions for a First Date." *OkCupid*, April 29, 2011. https://theblog.okcupid.com/the-best-questions-for-a-first-date-dba6adaa9df2.

Sanford, John. "Blood, Sweat and Fears: A Common Phobia's Odd Pathophysiology." *Stanford Medicine*, Spring 2013. http://sm.stanford.edu/archive/stanmed/2013spring/article6.html.

Sbravatti, Valerio. "Acoustic Startles in Horror Films." *Projections* 13, no. 1 (2019): 45–66. https://doi.org/10.3167/proj.2019.130104.

Schaller, Mark, and Justin H. Park. "The Behavioral Immune System (and Why It Matters)." *Current Directions in Psychological Science* 20, no. 2 (2011): 99–103. https://doi.org/10.1177/0963721411402596.

Scrivner, Coltan. "An Infectious Curiosity: Morbid Curiosity and Media Preferences during a Pandemic." *Evolutionary Studies in Imaginative Culture* 5, no. 1 (2020): 1–11. https://doi.org/10.26613/esic/5.1.206.

Scrivner, Coltan. "The Psychology of Morbid Curiosity: Development and Initial Validation of the Morbid Curiosity Scale." Preprint, under submission (2021). https://psyarxiv.com/xug34/.

Scrivner, Coltan, John A. Johnson, Jens Kjeldgaard-Christiansen, and Mathias Clasen. "Pandemic Practice: Horror Fans and Morbidly Curious Individuals Are More Psychologically Resilient during the Covid-19 Pandemic." *Personality and Individual Differences* 168, no. 1 (2021): 110397. https://doi.org/10.1016/j.paid.2020.110397.

Seery, Mark D., E. Alison Holman, and Roxane Cohen Silver. "Whatever Does Not Kill Us: Cumulative Lifetime Adversity, Vulnerability, and Resilience." *Journal of Personality and Social Psychology* 99, no. 6 (2010): 1025–41. https://doi.org/10.1037/a0021344.

Simone, Tiffany. "The Power of Horror Films as a Cure for Anxiety." *Medium.com*, July 22, 2018. https://medium.com/@tiffanysdillon/the-power-of-horror-films-as-cure-for-anxiety-e30830e0c2b1.

Simons, D., and W. R. Silveira. "Post-Traumatic Stress Disorder in Children after Television Programmes." *British Medical Journal* 308, no. 6925 (1994): 389–90. https://doi.org/10.1136/bmj.308.6925.389.

Simons, Ronald C. *Boo! Culture, Experience, and the Startle Reflex*. New York: Oxford University Press, 1996.

Sinnott, Joan M., H. Anton Speaker, Laura A. Powell, and Kelly W. Mosteller. "Perception of Scary Halloween Masks by Zoo Animals and Humans." *International Journal of Comparative Psychology* 25, no. 2 (2012): 83–96.

Siskel, Gene, and Roger Ebert. *Sneak Previews with Siskel and Ebert*. Public Broadcasting System, October 24, 1980.

Skal, David J. *The Monster Show: A Cultural History of Horror*. Rev. ed. New York: Faber and Faber, 2001.

Skenazy, Lenore. "It's Torture! It's Porn! What's Not to Like? Plenty, Actually." *AdAge*, May 28, 2007. https://adage.com/article/lenore-skenazy/torture-porn-plenty/116897.

Smith, Daniel, Philip Schlaepfer, Katie Major, Mark Dyble, Abigail E. Page, James Thompson, Nikhil Chaudhary, et al. "Cooperation and the Evolution of

Hunter-Gatherer Storytelling." *Nature Communications* 8, no. 1 (2017): 1853. https://doi.org/10.1038/s41467-017-02036-8.

Smith, Murray. *Film, Art, and the Third Culture: A Naturalized Aesthetics of Film.* Oxford: Oxford University Press, 2017.

Sparks, Glenn G. "The Prevalence and Intensity of Fright Reactions to Mass Media: Implications of the Activation-Arousal View." *Communication Quarterly* 37, no. 2 (1989): 108–17. https://doi.org/10.1080/01463378909385532.

Špinka, M., R. C. Newberry, and M. Bekoff. "Mammalian Play: Training for the Unexpected." *Quarterly Review of Biology* 76, no. 2 (2001): 141–68.

Steckenfinger, Shawn A., and Asif A. Ghazanfar. "Monkey Visual Behavior Falls into the Uncanny Valley." *Proceedings of the National Academy of Sciences* 106, no. 43 (2009): 18362–66. https://doi.org/10.1073/pnas.0910063106.

Steen, Francis F., and Stephanie A. Owens. "Evolution's Pedagogy: An Adaptationist Model of Pretense and Entertainment." *Journal of Cognition and Culture* 1, no. 4 (2001): 289–321.

Sternberg, Esther M. "Walter B. Cannon and '"Voodoo" Death': A Perspective from 60 Years On." *American Journal of Public Health* 92, no. 10 (2002): 1564–66. https://doi.org/10.2105/ajph.92.10.1564.

Sterpenich, Virginie, Lampros Perogamvros, Giulio Tononi, and Sophie Schwartz. "Fear in Dreams and in Wakefulness: Evidence for Day/Night Affective Homeostasis." *Human Brain Mapping* 41, no. 3 (2019): 840–50. https://doi.org/10.1002/hbm.24843.

Stritzke, Werner G. K., Christopher J. Patrick, and Alan R. Lang. "Alcohol and Human Emotion: A Multidimensional Analysis Incorporating Startle-Probe Methodology." *Journal of Abnormal Psychology* 104, no. 1 (1995): 114–22. https://doi.org/10.1037/0021-843x.104.1.114.

Stubbersfield, Joseph M., Emma G. Flynn, and Jamshid J. Tehrani. "Cognitive Evolution and the Transmission of Popular Narratives: A Literature Review and Application to Urban Legends." *Evolutionary Studies in Imaginative Culture* 1, no. 1 (2018): 121–36. https://doi.org/10.26613/esic/1.1.20.

"Student Dies of Shock While Watching Horror Films." *Times of India* (Hyderabad), December 6, 2010. https://timesofindia.indiatimes.com/city/hyderabad/Student-dies-of-shock-while-watching-horror-films/articleshow/7049952.cms.

Sturgeon, Theodore. "Books: On Hand." *Venture Science Fiction*, 1958, 66.

Subliminal Communication Technology: Hearing before the Subcommittee on Transportation, Aviation and Materials of the Committee on Science and Technology, U.S. House of Representatives, Ninety-Eighth Congress, Second Session. Washington, DC: US Government Printing Office, 1984. https://books.google.dk/books?id=vjosAAAAMAAJ.

Tamás, Viktória, Ferenc Kocsor, Petra Gyuris, Noémi Kovács, Endre Czeiter, and András Büki. "The Young Male Syndrome—an Analysis of Sex, Age, Risk Taking and Mortality in Patients with Severe Traumatic Brain Injuries." *Frontiers in Neurology* 10 (2019). https://doi.org/10.3389/fneur.2019.00366.

Tan, Ed S. *Emotion and the Structure of Narrative Film: Film as an Emotion Machine.* Hillsdale, NJ: Lawrence Erlbaum, 1996.

Trope, Yaacov, and Nira Liberman. "Construal-Level Theory of Psychological Distance." *Psychological Review* 117, no. 2 (2010): 440–63. https://doi.org/10.1037/a0018963.

Tybur, Joshua M., Debra Lieberman, Robert Kurzban, and Peter DeScioli. "Disgust: Evolved Function and Structure." *Psychological Review* 120, no. 1 (2013): 65–84. https://doi.org/10.1037/a0030778.

Valli, Katja, and Antti Revonsuo. "The Threat Simulation Theory in Light of Recent Empirical Evidence: A Review." *American Journal of Psychology* 122, no. 1 (2009): 17–38. http://www.ncbi.nlm.nih.gov/pubmed/19353929.

Visch, Valentijn T., Ed S. Tan, and Dylan Molenaar. "The Emotional and Cognitive Effect of Immersion in Film Viewing." *Cognition & Emotion* 24, no. 8 (2010): 1439–45. https://doi.org/10.1080/02699930903498186.

"Watching Horror Films Burns Nearly 200 Calories a Time." *The Telegraph* (London), October 28, 2012. https://www.telegraph.co.uk/news/uknews/9638876/Watching-horror-films-burns-nearly-200-calories-a-time.html.

Weisberg, Deena S., Paul Bloom, David M. Sobel, and Joshua Goodstein. "Young Children Are Reality-Prone When Thinking about Stories." *Journal of Cognition and Culture* 13, nos. 3–4 (2013): 383–407. https://doi.org/10.1163/15685373-12342100.

Weisberg, Deena S., and Alison Gopnik. "Pretense, Counterfactuals, and Bayesian Causal Models: Why What Is Not Real Really Matters." *Cognitive Science* 37, no. 7 (2013): 1368–81. https://doi.org/10.1111/cogs.12069.

Williams, Linda. "Film Bodies: Gender, Genre, and Excess." *Film Quarterly* 44, no. 4 (1991): 2–13. https://doi.org/10.2307/1212758. www.jstor.org/stable/1212758.

Wilson, Barbara J. "The Effects of Two Control Strategies on Children's Emotional Reactions to a Frightening Movie Scene." *Journal of Broadcasting & Electronic Media* 33, no. 4 (1989): 397–418. https://doi.org/10.1080/08838158909364091.

Wilson, Barbara J. "Media and Children's Aggression, Fear, and Altruism." *Future of Children* 18, no. 1 (2008): 87–118. https://doi.org/10.1353/foc.0.0005.

Wood, Robin. "An Introduction to the American Horror Film." In *American Nightmare: Essays on the Horror Film*, edited by Andrew Britton, Richard Lippe, Tony Williams, and Robin Wood, 7–28. Toronto: Festival of Festivals, 1979.

Woods, Rebecca. "*Ghostwatch*: The BBC Spoof That Duped a Nation." *BBC News*, October 30, 2017. https://www.bbc.com/news/uk-england-41740176.

Wright, John C., Aletha C. Huston, Alice Leary Reitz, and Suwatchara Piemyat. "Young Children's Perceptions of Television Reality: Determinants and Developmental Differences." *Developmental Psychology* 30, no. 2 (1994): 229–39. https://doi.org/10.1037/0012-1649.30.2.229.

Wühr, Peter, Benjamin P. Lange, and Sascha Schwarz. "Tears or Fears? Comparing Gender Stereotypes about Movie Preferences to Actual Preferences." *Frontiers in Psychology* 8 (2017). https://doi.org/10.3389/fpsyg.2017.00428.

Xygalatas, Dimitris, Sammyh Khan, Martin Lang, Radek Kundt, Eva Kundtová-Klocová, Jan Krátký, and John Shaver. "Effects of Extreme Ritual Practices on Psychophysiological Well-Being." *Current Anthropology* 60, no. 5 (2019): 699–707. https://doi.org/10.1086/705665.

Xygalatas, Dimitris, Panagiotis Mitkidis, Ronald Fischer, Paul Reddish, Joshua Skewes, Armin W. Geertz, Andreas Roepstorff, and Joseph Bulbulia. "Extreme Rituals Promote Prosociality." *Psychological Science* 24, no. 8 (2013): 1602–5. https://doi.org/10.1177/0956797612472910.

Yoo, Seung-Schik, Ninad Gujar, Peter Hu, Ferenc A. Jolesz, and Matthew P. Walker. "The Human Emotional Brain without Sleep—a Prefrontal Amygdala Disconnect." *Current Biology* 17, no. 20 (2007): R877–R878. https://doi.org/10.1016/j.cub.2007.08.007.

Zarrelli, Natalie. "How the Hidden Sounds of Horror Movie Soundtracks Freak You Out." *Atlas Obscura*, October 31, 2016. https://www.atlasobscura.com/articles/how-the-hidden-sounds-of-horror-movie-soundtracks-freak-you-out.

Zillmann, Dolf, and James B. Weaver III. "Gender-Socialization Theory of Reactions to Horror." In *Horror Films: Current Research on Audience Preferences and Reactions*, edited by James B. Weaver III and Ron Tamborini, 81–101. New York: Routledge, 1996.

Zillmann, Dolf, James B. Weaver III, Norbert Mundorf, and Charles F. Aust. "Effects of an Opposite-Gender Companion's Affect to Horror on Distress, Delight, and Attraction." *Journal of Personality and Social Psychology* 51, no. 3 (1986): 586–94. https://doi.org/10.1037/0022-3514.51.3.586.

Zinoman, Jason. "Jordan Peele on a Truly Terrifying Monster: Racism." *New York Times*, February 16, 2017. https://www.nytimes.com/2017/02/16/movies/jordan-peele-interview-get-out.html.

Zinoman, Jason. *Shock Value: How a Few Eccentric Outsiders Gave Us Nightmares, Conquered Hollywood, and Invented Modern Horror.* New York: Penguin, 2011.

Zuckerman, Marvin. *Behavioral Expressions and Biosocial Bases of Sensation Seeking.* New York: Cambridge University Press, 1994.

Index

For the benefit of digital users, indexed terms that span two pages (e.g., 52–53) may, on occasion, appear on only one of those pages.

Figures and boxes are indicated by *f* and *b* following the page number